Coming Together

Healing the political divide and finding the humanity in those that disagree with us

Sean McCutcheon

Sean McCutcheon

Library of Congress Control Number: 2022914364

Contents

Foreword

We are being divided and convinced to hate one another, and we must stop that from happening. The purpose of this book is to help you see the humanity in people with a different opinion than your own. Over the years, I have seen a divide grow in this country between people on multiple fronts, including religion, race, and political ideology.

We have become engulfed in numerous conflicts where we do not see each other as people and have come to believe the worst about those different from us. I want to halt that division and bring us back together. There is much we agree on, but many people profit from us, remaining apart or hoping that we are so overcome by despair that we do not take action to fix things.

During the course of this book, I will be talking about serious topics and making some serious points, but I will try to do so in a compassionate fashion. I will not assign blame or fault in most cases because I am looking for a way forward, and I would like for us to do that together. However, there will be a few times where I will be looking at one side or the other almost exclusively to do the heavy lifting on a topic.

I started this book a few days after the 2020 presidential election in the United States, with Biden being declared president and Trump refusing to concede. Throughout this election cycle, I've spent a lot of time reflecting on how Trump received so much support during his presidency and what can be done to reconcile the differences that were exacerbated during his presidency but have been steadily worsening over time.

I am sure many people would like to lay the blame solely at Trump's feet for this division and move on, but life is never that simple. Rather this division has been festering for a while, and numerous people enjoy exploiting these divisions to profit from our hatred and fear of one another or to use it for political gain. Plus, these exploiters tend to get the added benefit of avoiding any of the consequences of kicking over the anthill by stirring us up.

With that in mind, I will be talking a lot about some of the issues we disagree on and how we can find some common ground with those issues. I will not focus solely on who is responsible for exploiting our divisions; there are plenty of books blaming people for our current predicament. Most of them are not productive or conducive to solving our problems. I want to focus on resolving these problems and finding a way forward together.

Introduction

As with any new book, the reader's first thought is, "Do I want to read this?" It is each author's responsibility to help them make an informed decision about their book. So let me help with this decision as this book is not for everyone. It is mainly for the people who have felt we have lost control of the political discourse, those that have felt excluded in this discourse. It is for the people who want to make a change, those who are tired of being told that because someone disagrees with us, they are our enemy. It is for the people that understand that we are not a monolith.

Conversely, and I think just as importantly, this book is not for some people. It is not for the gatekeepers, and neither is it for the trolls. The gatekeepers believe that you must conform to all of a group's beliefs to be accepted as a member, which leads them not to challenge their thoughts and ideas. They believe in cancelling people that don't perfectly align with their moral views. The trolls just want to cause chaos and trouble. They just want to make people angry. They want to lie to you and misguide you. Neither one of these groups wants discourse. Neither one wants us to see someone that disagrees with us as fully developed humans.

This book is for bridge builders. If you are tired of being told that the other side completely lacks humanity, then this is for you. If your media feeds are filled with nothing but despair telling you that there is nothing to be done, then this book is for you. Now, this is not filled with sunshine and rainbows. I will address difficult topics and, when I can, try to devise a course of action to help resolve an issue or at least help you see the other side.

There has been a trend that has been bothering me for a while now. Many of us have been insulated from people we disagree with or who may have a different opinion, and it has been getting worse. Many people are afraid or in pain, and we are having a hard time seeing that. Some people have lost hope.

But instead of dealing with that pain and despair, we are distracted into thinking their pain is a lie. Even worse, we are sometimes told that other people trying to heal are causing us pain. I hope this book helps you realize that just because people disagree with you does not mean they are your enemy. That when they try to fix an injustice that does not infringe upon you. I would love it if we eventually saw each other as an ally in resolving the issues we all face.

To illustrate the point of this book, that we are stronger together, I will start this off with a story. In late 2020 and early 2021, hedge funds were shorting the stock of the companies GameStop and AMC to make a lot of money. This process would have ensured that both companies died. However, in early 2021, many people came together to prevent billionaires from destroying those companies and hopefully make a little money while they were doing it. No one cared what beliefs each person had when trying to save these companies; they came together and stood up against these billionaires.

Afterward, many billionaires took to television and other media to express their displeasure about how they had been prevented from earning more money and that the rules needed to be changed so that commoners could not prevent them from earning billions by destroying companies again. The media gave these billionaires lots of airplay, and politicians from both sides wanted to understand what happened. They agreed that people should not be allowed to interfere in this process again.

Let me reiterate that lots and lots of normal people came together and stopped billionaires from destroying a few companies, and when they did that, the media demonized the people. Politicians wanted to take away the power from the regular people. These people worked together towards a common goal. They made a change; they were noticed.

The billionaires did not gain as much as they would like, but what about these regular people that actually made some money? What did they spend their money on? Bills, education, some gave to charity. These regular people took the money they earned and put it into their economies, while the billionaires that did not make as much money derided them.

We have more power than we know. We are not as separate from the other side as we are led to believe. If we work together, we can change the world. They know that, and so should we.

I, like many of us, am scared of the direction that this country is heading. However, unlike many, I am not afraid of one side or the other. I am more afraid that we are being convinced to hate each other. I am more afraid that we see each other as the enemy, and it is getting easier and easier to isolate ourselves. This allows us to believe the lies we are told and prevents us from working together.

We are told to divide and keep ourselves separate from one another. Today's world also makes this so much easier. Not only does our media do its best to divide us and tell us the evils of the other side, but our social media also makes it easy to make an insulated bubble of thought that prevents dissenting opinions from entering.

A pandemic was thrown on top of all this, ensuring that we maintained a literal physical distance does not help the matter. However, we are more alike than we realize at times. We mostly agree on the problems facing our society, and both of us have good (and some bad) ideas on how to fix them. I want us to see the humanity in each other, and I want us to see the pain that the other is feeling, and I want us to heal the pain that we are going through.

I am tired of all the lies that we tell each other. I am tired of unintentionally spreading lies that I've been told. I am tired of all of the lies that are being spread about my beliefs. I am tired of all the lies being told about those who don't share my beliefs. I am tired of the lies.

This is my attempt to tell some truths that need to be said. We need to hear each other more. We are all in pain and are all surprised when we find out that someone else is hurting too. We also do not ever want to think that our actions are causing other people pain, but sometimes they do, intentionally or not.

What can we do to fix these problems? That's a great question. This book will tackle some of the problem areas and provide us with some places to start. More importantly, I know that many of us also want to fix these problems, and I want you to know, first and foremost, that none of us is alone.

Before the healing can begin in any process, truths have to be acknowledged. A light has to be shown upon the injury before healing can begin. However, in today's day and age, it is hard to see the truth. This is because it is so hard to tell what is true anymore. Especially since so many people make money off of lying to us and convincing us to hate one another and that we are what is wrong with this country.

I know that the most common rebuttal to being told that people make money off of dividing us is to say that we are trying to start a culture war. But what these people intentionally neglect to mention is that we are already in one, and we are losing. So, yes, we, all of us, the people that agree and those that disagree with you.

Because as long as we fight each other, we are not fighting to improve things. As long as we think that the opposite side is the problem, we are not dealing with the things making our lives difficult. There has been a long history of rich people telling poor and middle-class people that really poor people are the problem.

Now, before you think I want to burn it all down and start over, just know I do not. There is a lot of good that we have all achieved together, and many good things have happened in our country. So, while I want significant changes, I don't want to bring the system down. That only hurts the people at the bottom.

To illustrate this dichotomy, I am excited about the achievements of some of the wealthiest people in this country. Not just happy, I am excited for them and want them to continue to achieve success. My wife and I both have Amazon Prime accounts. Jeff Bezos worked amazingly hard to make his dreams a reality. Mark Zuckerberg has made a company that allows us to come closer together. They made amazing companies that have changed the face of the world. They have changed our discourse about energy independence, privacy, and interconnectedness.

Now while I think that their accomplishments should be praised, I also think that Amazon workers deserve bathroom breaks and that Facebook needs to work better to ensure our privacy and remove dangerously misleading articles. All because I think one thing is true does not mean I cannot think the other is true. You can hold two truths about something at once.

The most painful truth is that the changes, whether in viewpoint or action, will be difficult. Change always is. But as many of us know, there is only one way out: to assess the situation we find ourselves in honestly. This is something that we can do together. I hope that you see that we have more in common than we have that separates us. Additionally, I hope you see that some problems require input from all of us to make something even better.

To hit a couple more hard ones before we move forward, and if you take anything away from this entire effort, please let it be this: those on the left and right of the political spectrum care very deeply about this country, and neither of them wants to destroy it. If there is a second thing, your ideas are valid without invalidating their ideas; in fact, working together can make a better result for everyone. Lastly, a lot of people make money off of telling us lies and sowing division between us. Don't let this work.

Have you seen how the Clintons, Bushs, and Obamas get along? Despite their massive political differences, they genuinely love and respect one another. They have a lot in common that goes beyond their political differences. They have a shared experience that bonds them. Many of you have bonds with people that disagree with you. Many of you have family or people you love that have different ideas.

As a personal example, everyone reviewing this book for me disagrees with me about something I will write; at least one of them will disagree with that sentence out of spite, and they definitely disagree with one another. However, we have shared experiences that created a bond that lets us see past those differences of opinion. Even if we view things from a different political light, the value they bring to my life far outweighs any difference of opinion. I value their input and insight, even though we think that the other one is wrong when solving the problems we face as Americans.

If there is one thing I want us to take away from this, we need to recognize the basic humanity in one another. There are lots of forces trying to drive wedges between us. Do not allow that. Build bridges. There is more that unites us.

I started writing this shortly after the 2020 election. This election served to highlight the growing differences in the U. S. along political lines, which reinvigorated my desire to write a book to reconcile those differences. I've had this idea a few times over the decades, and this recent election highlighted the need for me to try and reach out to both sides. However, these past few years have really hit a boiling point with some of the issues that have gone on, and it is time to learn to work together. I think that we have a lot to offer one another and including each other's ideas and concerns in the discussion is necessary.

Let's start with a reminder; we have more in common than what separates us. Many of you have a shared history or bond with someone that disagrees with you. You know each other to be decent, hard-working, honest people. Some may rationalize this as thinking this person is not emblematic of the other side of the spectrum. You may joke and tease each other, but you still trust each other. Notice that you share a lot of the same values and have a lot in common; it's just that you want to solve the problems faced by society differently.

If you do not have someone like that in your life, that is something that I want to focus on later in the book. Both sides have ways of maintaining their bubble of thought, some of which are the same, and some are different. Either way, they should be acknowledged so you can hear different ideas.

You should not lose friends just because they disagree with you politically. Now, I understand your concern that the other side is being portrayed in the media as being full of Nazis or Anarchists, and to be fair, there are plenty of those. But think about the people you know in your life that you disagree with, are they that way? Did you accept someone into your life that wants to kill everyone or burn everything down? Probably not. All because you disagree with someone on how to solve an issue does not negate the basic humanity within them.

I want to discuss this difference in viewpoints and opinions so you can learn more about the other side. I want you to remember that there are people that differ from you that you care about, and frankly, you can both be right at the same time. Here is where you can get the most work done to benefit everyone.

So what topics am I going to write about? Gun rights? Healthcare? Abortion? The Media? Yes. To all of it and a few more. Why? Because I see so many of us being manipulated around these topics, I want people to realize it. Because then we can move forward and work together to solve the problems.

Sometimes solving a problem starts with an uncomfortable discussion. However, we first need to realize that this is not a team sport where it's Democrat vs. Republican. This is not a football game. This is not a situation where one team has to win and the other has to lose. We can all win.

Lastly, just a heads up, I will end each section with an ask. Each section will have a part where I ask you to do something to improve this discourse. Do not worry; you will not hate them all; at one point, I ask you to take your friends shooting so they can see how much fun they can have.

Chapter One

Profiting from Our Division

Initially, I didn't want to name who benefited financially or politically from dividing us, but the more time went on, the more I felt that was disingenuous. It is essential to know who would want to divide us and why. Therefore, we can hold these people accountable and do so appropriately. Plus, this means we can stop falling for their traps.

Because of the level of violence that has permeated the political sphere recently, let me be clear when I say accountable. We can hold them to the truth. Politicians can be voted out; they can be petitioned. You can change the channel, either literally or figuratively, from different media platforms. You can log out of social media platforms. It is this level of accountability that I am talking about. The power of your vote, both at the ballot and with your wallet, should not be underestimated. In fact, these forms of accountability are so powerful that they have changed the world.

One final time, because of some recent acts of violence, I want to clarify that is not what I mean. In fact, if someone says that you should use violence to get what you want, they are an instigator, and if you follow through on violent acts, you are a criminal. Also, if someone says that the other side is always using violence to make their point and you should fear for their lives, you should probably change the channel. While there are some violent people on both sides, most people are peaceful.

The first two sections of this part of the book are more of a scene-setting for what follows. The next sections are about the two political parties we have and the inherent problems within them, followed by two sections about the media and how it contributes to all of this. Lastly, we will discuss how we can reclaim our power.

Chapter Two

The American Political Environment

Before we talk about the specifics of the diversity of political thought within the U.S., let's cover what the entire spectrum looks like. There are two axes to political thought; we all know about the polarity of left and right. Most of the political discourse we see and participate in is along those lines. However, another axis that is not discussed as frequently is that of authoritarian and libertarian, the rule of the government vs. the rule of the person.

To start with the first axis, left and right, the U.S. has a very stunted view of this. Our politicians tend to skew to the right. Even our most "radically leftist" politicians barely crack the moderate scale of this axis by proposing policies that every other industrialized nation already has in place, some of which the U.S. used to have. Now those on the left and the right disagree on a wide variety of topics, but basically, the divide on this spectrum consists of whether you believe that society should be more egalitarian (left) or hierarchical (right).

The other axis, authoritarian vs. libertarian, tends to get conflated with the first. This has to do with the role of government at large, with a more authoritarian government telling the populace what they can and cannot do, with a libertarian government allowing more freedoms. A prevalent misconception in U.S. political discourse is that both the left and right want an authoritarian government. How intentional this is up for debate.

Now let's talk about the overlap between our political parties and why we are so frustrated with the current system. In case you haven't been paying attention over the last few decades, both those on the left and libertarians have become increasingly frustrated with our elected officials. That's because the only option available during most presidential elections has been between an authoritarian on the right with a blue tie (and can talk to the left) and an authoritarian on the right with a red tie. Of course, there are plenty of leftists and libertarians that never liked Biden or Obama, and there are plenty of libertarians that never liked Trump. But authoritarians liked all of them.

Our political parties, both of them, tend to skew towards authoritarian leaders regardless of who is in office. If you do not believe me, look at the increasing number of executive orders presidents have made. For example, how many people were furious with the number of executive orders that Obama, Trump, or Biden made during their presidencies. These practices would naturally upset either those on the left or libertarian. However, they are not actual law, they have not gone through congress, and for those not paying attention, that is the problem, no matter who is president.

In fairness, a lot of the blame for the increase in executive orders can be placed squarely on the legislative branch and its inability to pass legislation. However, we should be worried if our government is not working to the point that executive orders are required to do anything. We will discuss how to fix these problems later, as it is fairly complex and multifaceted.

We should all be upset that our government no longer seems to work for the people. A completely non-functioning government, regardless of size, does not help anyone. Going back and forth between parties signing executive orders doesn't solve any of our problems and makes our government seem like a joke.

This behavior by our politicians really does then limit the political landscape to a choice between Red and Blue, without giving a variety of thought. They are behaving in a manner in which there is not only a hierarchy (right), but they are above the populace they serve (authoritarian). Anyone with ideas that are libertarian or to the left gets silenced in this environment. Even moderates from either axis aren't allowed to participate in the process. These groups have great ideas, but they are not allowed to participate.

Our political choices should not have devolved into Red vs. Blue. Political thought is much broader than what we have in our political system. However, this devolution does provide us with the illusion of choice.

This whole effort of making it seem like we have a choice in political leadership works out well for those the system empowers but does not work out well for the vast majority of us, you and I included. We do not truly get representation, and that is a problem. It's also a problem that many other people do not get representation.

One thing I've heard from people is their frustration with those who vote for a political party like it's a sports team. They're always loyal to their party no matter what their party is doing. Ironically, they may even be accurate at describing problems within the opposite political party, but they are terrible at identifying the problems within their own.

This isn't a team sport, though. We need to remember that we are all on the same team. We must remember that politicians work for us; they are not in charge of us.

I'm sure that many of us see this line of thinking with many of our friends on both sides of the political spectrum. They see one party as absolute evil and can not see the problems within their own party. This leads us to some dangerous lines of thought.

I see some on the left spreading memes implying that the right is all Nazis, Fascists, or Confederates that want to destroy America. Alternatively, I see some on the right spreading memes implying that all those on the left want free stuff to take all of your guns and destroy America.

This harms our political discourse by creating an environment where we no longer see those that disagree with us as people. This isolates us from one another and prevents those with differing opinions from being able to engage. I will be talking more about how we can fix this later.

There are lots of people across the full political spectrum that do not line up with either party. I mentioned the full spectrum with both axes because our population covers the gambit. Those that we call the left would be considered moderate or conservative elsewhere in the world, and those on the right have, especially recently, skewed far to the right in recent years.

I know this may come as a surprise, but it's true. The U.S. stands as the sole developed country that does not have universal healthcare, and we have decided to move away from being the world leader in environmental efforts. Even our politicians don't work together anymore.

Now it would be nice to say: Let's have (at least) 4 political parties! We now have the two authoritarian right parties and a Progressive and Libertarian party. That would help people get the representation they seek, and it would be harder for corporate lobbyists to buy votes. Additionally, it would help address specific problems that certain groups may need.

But that is an unrealistic expectation in the short term. So, we have to work with what we currently have. On the plus side, we will discuss actions we can take to fix our current political environment.

Another thing of note, lots of people are enforcing "political purity" tests for our groups, excluding those that do not line up with a smaller subset of ideologies. This is made easier with the media we consume and how we engage and are engaged with social media. This makes it easier for politicians to line up with their own political purity.

This leads to what is known as the "Iron Law of Institutions," coined by Jon Schwarz. This is when people care most about their power within an institution rather than the institution itself. As this pertains to politics, it means that Republican and Democrat politicians do what is needed to remain in power within the party rather than what is best for the people. I know that many of us see within the "other" party, but it happens with many politicians.

This leads to the first ask for this section: to get rid of the gatekeepers. There is plenty of room for diversity of thought within our existing political parties, and we should not allow these people to exclude ideas just to enrich the party's power at the country's expense.

This applies to both parties, and those on the left and right do this in force, and it needs to stop. I know that some will argue that they will not stop excluding people because they will never give in to tyranny, but the problem is that both ends of the political spectrum end in tyranny, just of different types. Just because someone disagrees with you does not mean they will ensure we descend into a tyrannical rule. In fact, the best way to prevent a descent into tyranny is to work together. This will prevent the worst aspects of either party from taking control.

The second ask is a little multi-faceted. The first part is joining a smaller political party that aligns with your values, especially at a local level. Once that party has enough clout, start going for state positions and eventually federal. The next is to hold our national leaders responsible and have them work together. This country is accustomed to grassroots movements. This type of change can only start from that direction.

To take this in a different direction, let's look at something we have in common. Most of us like term limits, but let's face it, those in power love being in power for as long as possible; see the law mentioned above. Why would they not? With that and gerrymandering, they get to pick who votes for them, and they stay in power forever.

Think about this, how nice would it be to get rid of Nancy Pelosi or Mitch McConnell? Spoiler alert, I know many of us also want to get them out of office. So, we have that in common.

At least one of the reasons we want to get rid of them is the same. They both keep things stagnant, and that's a bad thing in a swamp. This touches on why I wanted to write this; despite the fact that they both have a lot in common, they retain power by keeping us at odds with one another. They're not representing our best interests, and we have allies everywhere that want to help you develop a long-term fix for the issue.

Please notice that I keep pointing out similarities between the multiple groups because we have more in common than we have apart. Of course, that will not always be the case for every topic throughout this book, but where I do not think we can agree, I will try to offer a way to work together.

Additionally, one major point of agreement is our need to "get money out of politics." Two recent Supreme Court battles have allowed money to get further entrenched in politics; the most well-known of these is the Citizens United decision.

This declared that corporations were people and that they could contribute unlimited funds to politicians.

This has brought far more money into politics and allowed corruption to occur legally. Even while I can see the constitutional arguments that allow this decision to take place, the results have led to a lot of harm to our political system, which our legislature couldn't fix. Unfortunately, they feel no political pressure to fix the situation. In fact, quite the opposite, the current environment allows them to collect a lot of money for themselves.

So, I ask that we collaborate to repair the system. Many of our ideas are similar, such as term limits and getting money out of politics to repair the system. If we work together, then both political parties will have to listen to the will of the collective people.

Chapter Three

The Role of Government

With the concept of what our political spectrum looks like and what we can do to improve the overall environment, let's move on to discuss the specific role of government. Because it will have an impact on everything else we discuss in the book, we all have strong opinions about what it should be.

What do we want our government to look like? What is the primary purpose of each level, such as local, state, and federal? Well, let's look at what they were tasked with doing.

First, state governments wield considerable power over our daily lives. They implement policies that directly and immediately impact our taxes, roads, schools, emergency services, relief work, and what actions we are permitted to take. Furthermore, due to the way our system is set up, these policies do not have to match up across states, and in many cases, they don't.

To be fair, this is why we are called the United States. We also identify a lot with which state we are from. The federal government was designed to make sure that the states all play together, handle foreign relations, and address concerns that affected citizens in numerous states. Since our country's inception, the government's dynamics have changed to allow for a stronger federal government.

There has always been a push and pull between the power dynamics of the federal and state governments. Particularly with regards to who has the power to do what. Because of the ebb and flow of this power structure, we have ended up with a federal government with more power than it initially started with. Some of it was because states gave up power and authority, and some because the federal government said that states could no longer take specific actions, like enslaving people.

This consolation has led to some good. We now can have a more unified vision for the country. Plus, when we want to take on monumental tasks, like going to the moon, or Mars, we can collectively make that happen. We have also used this authority to generate revenue streams allowing richer states to help poorer states take care of their citizens.

However, a stronger federal government does have some downsides because, as I've alluded to, once the government gets the power, it tends to hold onto it. It is this problem that a lot of people are concerned about. But unfortunately, many people are only concerned about the government's power when the party they disagree with is in power. However, that doesn't mean that there shouldn't be limits on the extent and types of power the government should have, especially regarding our personal freedoms and choices.

Many of us are concerned about government overreach in our lives. Many of us are concerned about the government surveilling U.S. citizens or involvement in foreign countries. Most of us agree that there need to be term limits, and those with gross ethical violations, such as making millions off insider trading or covering up sexual abuse, should not be allowed to hold office.

We start to disagree on the size of government, particularly with which part of the government we're talking about. For example, many people worried that President Obama, and now Biden, would allow unidentified government agents to take their guns.

However, during the summer of 2020, when unidentified government agents were attacking and arresting protesters in the U.S., the exact thing that these same people were afraid of, they were grateful that these unidentified government agents were violating the civil rights of the protestors.

Conversely, many people say "all cops are bastards" but expect the police to handle all of the problems within their community. Hypocrisy is not limited to one group.

Here is the point that we all need to remember. Once you give the government power, it keeps that power. So, if we give the government power over one group of people, there is a good chance that the government will also use that power against other groups.

Because the truth is, if you want to use the government to hurt people, it can also be used to hurt you. There are far too many examples of this to list here, but the most newsworthy of the last couple of decades has been the Patriot Act, which, among other things, significantly expanded the government's authority to collect information against U.S. citizens.

People tend to get upset when reminded about this collection, but both parties have continued to renew this policy for decades. So, we must decide if we want our government to take away the rights of its citizens. Unfortunately, the answer to that has been "yes" far too frequently. But we can change that.

Conversely, there are wonderful things that the government has done for the people. We, mostly, enjoy having the use of roads, police, the fire department, public schools, and the military. Plus, there are very popular programs that many Americans rely upon for support, like Social Security, Medicare,

Medicaid, and Food Stamps. How many people in our lives use these programs?

We will delve into specific issues later, but for now, think about the role of government at large. The U.S. is a government of the people, by the people, and for the people. All sides of the political spectrum (left, right, libertarian, and authoritarian) have argued this point in massive protests over the past year. We all wanted to remind the government that they work for us, not the other way around.

Every side of the political spectrum made the same complaint, even if it was about different things. But instead of finding a way to support one another and find a way forward, we were told about how the "other" side was wrong. Because if we are convinced that we can support each other, we can hold the government accountable, which means that there are a lot of incentives to convince us that the other side is not human and how afraid we should be of them. We should not be afraid of people disagreeing with us. We are stronger together.

Moving back to the government of the people, we are all concerned that it has been taken away from us over the years. This is true; although some of us were never represented by the government, it does not have to remain this way. We can make the government work for us again. I know that we have all said harsh things about it in the past, but when you look at individual programs, we are very supportive, and some of us need those benefits to survive.

There have been times in our history when the government has undertaken large projects to benefit some citizens. Like the Homestead Act or the creation of the GI Bill. Both allowed some citizens to create a home or get an education. In addition, a lot of our infrastructure was built using government assistance. As I mentioned earlier, many of us have people in our lives who have benefited from government programs such as Medicare and Medicaid.

Earlier I also mentioned Social Security and unemployment benefits, but those are slightly different. Medicare and Medicaid are paid by all of us to ensure that those that need those services have access to them. Not all of us may end up using them, but they are there if we need them.

Unemployment benefits are different; this is insurance that is paid to cover possible job loss. Like any insurance, we hope we will not need it. However, if we do, then it should be there. Again, if the government says there isn't enough money for unemployment benefits, it's the same as the insurance provider we've been paying, saying they don't want to pay us for the service they've already taken the money for.

One thing that we can do is stop acting like the presidential election is the Superbowl of government leadership. While the President is an important symbol who can present a vision of what they want for the U.S., there are a few points to remember: the U.S. president does not have that much power by design, and there are numerous other positions that have far more impact upon your life than the president does.

The local county board has more power over our day-to-day lives than the president. There are a lot of governmental positions that should have our attention. Too often, we ask our governors or president to answer questions that a local school board would better address.

So, the first round of asks here is to pay attention to and participate in local politics, whether learning more about and participating in local school boards or how the sheriff handles issues. For example, during one of the last elections for my local sheriff, I lined up politically with the guy that lost, but I knew the incumbent sheriff had saved the life of a dear friend's father. So, for me, it was a win-win scenario. Either way, I got someone who would care for the local population.

In addition, while I cared about who won the governorship in my state, I was more concerned about the local school board. Because while one would have an impact on the overall state, the other directly impacted my children on a day-to-day basis.

This is not a request to get you to run for office, but if you want to, please do. We need more diversity in our government; too many of them are lawyers, which doesn't represent the normal members of the population. Any homogenous group wouldn't be able to represent our diverse views as a community.

This is a request for all of us to find out more about what is happening at a local level. Get engaged because this will affect your day-to-day life. Where are stop signs located? How much money does the school have in its budget, and how are they spending it? If the poor kids within our communities can not afford lunch, should we pay for those lunches, or should we let them go hungry? Some choose to let children go hungry; should we accept that?

Next, we need to be more involved in our state governments. In the U.S., again by design, states have much control over things that affect our daily lives. There are a couple of examples that illustrate this point. When Mitt Romney was the governor of Massachusetts, he passed a healthcare plan to provide coverage for everyone in the state. This plan was actually the roadmap for the Affordable Care Act.

For reference, Massachusetts does not break into the top 10 states with the highest GDP, yet they were able to do this. Additionally, California is known to be both a haven for liberals and has a GDP equivalent to Great Britain. They also have a healthcare plan and taxpayer-funded pre-kindergarten for residents that qualify.

At a state level, there are a lot of things that we can agree upon. We may disagree on the federal tax rate for top earners, but we can both agree that the potholes have to be fixed. We both live in these communities; we can work together.

Now onto the federal government, this is where we see a lot of disagreement, and there are a lot of good reasons on both sides. Some of which we will delve into later in the book.

The next two sections of the book will discuss how each party profits off our divisions and address how we can help them reform into parties for the people. Because while having only two political parties that are supposed to work for the people is not ideal and does not represent the full spectrum of thought, the U.S. has zero political parties that function for the people, which is even less than ideal.

There is enough blame for both political parties and enough work to go around for us to improve the situation. Those who used to be aligned with a political party, or those calling themselves independent, will recognize some of the issues that I will be bringing up and may be some of the reasons why they left that party. In the next two sections, we will also talk about the political parties and their inherent problems.

Along those lines, people are really upset with the established political system. I will get into some specifics with each party later, but most people on both ends of the spectrum can see what these parties have become; it is pretty obvious. So, they are very frustrated with that and want things to change.

People once had faith in our government and wished for that trust to return. There are politicians out there that want us to be able to trust our government; unfortunately, there are so many more that just want to maintain the status quo of our system.

Some people have a hard time seeing why Trump was so popular, but I get it. Not only is he really good at selling a brand himself, but he promised to shake up the establishment in a way that hadn't been in a while. He promised a level of change that no one else was talking about. His opposition only offered a status quo, not a change, and definitely not an improvement.

When he ran for office, there were lots of people hurting and in desperation. Many of whom had been failed by the system. So, when given a choice between someone that is a huge part of that system, or someone who promises to tear it down, they choose the latter.

The system was not, and still is not, working for millions of Americans. The people looked at the two parties and saw how little they had been doing for regular people, and they decided they needed to shake up the establishment. That is why Bernie was, and is, so popular with many Americans.

The Democrats, fearing a shakeup of the establishment, went with establishment candidates in 2016 and 2020. People that would do everything to ensure the status quo. A status quo that has, actively or passively, hurt millions of Americans. That is why Trump was elected. He was elected to shake up the status quo and hopefully get the government working for the people again.

Unfortunately, he was not as effective at coming up with sound policies as he was with just shaking the establishment, which is why he lost in 2020 to the most established candidate, Biden. Unlike with Trump's election, things calmed down, but like Trump's presidency, what has changed? People are still hurting, and we all want change.

The point I am trying to make is that the problems highlighted and spotlighted under Trump still exist under Biden. Policies that were put in place by Trump that were deemed inhumane remain in effect under Biden. Trump may have been a bad president, but that does not make Biden a good one.

Alternatively, Gov. Cuomo was hailed by many during the pandemic. But when it came out that he misled the public on COVID case numbers and his treatment of staff, some of the same people that hailed him said that they weren't surprised and that anyone that knew New York politics knew he was a bad person. But why did they put him on a pedestal then? Trump may have been the loudest politician that did inappropriate things, but he was not the only one. People see the contradiction.

Compounding this problem, both parties have been actively trying to clean their houses of members that are not ideological purists. They are both working hard to make sure that the status quo is being maintained, a status quo that is hurting people and ensures that nothing gets done. Many of us are furious about this, and everyone knows it.

Then to make sure that we are ineffectual at making any change, we pointed at one another as being the cause of our problems. That is false. Your neighbor is not your enemy. How many of us have different political beliefs than our neighbors How often does that stop us from inviting them to a cookout, COVID notwithstanding? It does not stop me, and I know it does not stop my neighbors from inviting me. However, there are plenty of other reasons not to invite me, mainly because of my personality.

My biggest ask for this is to stop fighting one another and start fighting alongside one another. Politics is not a zero-sum game. All because one side wins does not mean that the other side loses. We can work together to improve our country and accomplish things that benefit people. We can make the drastic change we want to see in this world.

Chapter Four

The Republican Party and the Politics of Fear

Let me make something clear from the get-go. For this section, I am talking about the Republican party itself. I know that members of the right tend to skew towards the Republican party currently, but I am taking a break from talking about the right or left and instead want to focus on the party.

This section is not focused on policy issues; those remain to be addressed later. If you are a Republican, this section focuses on getting your house in order, as the next section will be about Democrats.

Currently, the Republican party is interested in making you afraid. Afraid that Democrats are stealing the election. Afraid of voter fraud, but only when they lose. Afraid that people are coming for your guns. Afraid that you will be taxed to poverty. Afraid that people fleeing violence without possessions will take your jobs. Afraid of the very government.

They would rather have you afraid that Dr. Seuss is being cancelled because of 'woke culture' than have you pay attention to their efforts to rewrite history books by removing references to slavery and how atrocious it was. They would rather have you worry about fake election fraud than gerrymandering. They want you to be afraid so that you don't notice their steps to stay in power.

They do know that fear has always been a huge motivator for people. They want to retain power and make you afraid of what the government might do to you. Plus, if they show incompetence within the government, this helps them ensure that they do not have to do anything to solve your problems. In fact, they can portray themselves as brave defenders against the same government they want to manage.

The current Republican party is very different from the Republican party that used to exist. They are the party that implemented the Environmental Protection Agency, and they are the ones that led the effort to repair the hole in the ozone layer. They had, and frankly still do have, a great track record of getting things done.

Unfortunately, they have been taken over by obstructionists, both to work on actual policy and on ensuring voter's rights. This is a huge problem that they are making a central part of their party's platform instead of trying to rectify.

They are actively working to prevent the government from properly functioning rather than work on policy from their perspectives. Think about it, when Democrats are in power, the debt ceiling is a problem, but not when the Republicans hold the reins. Or when a Republican governor passes healthcare legislation for their state, it's a good thing, but the same law applied to the country is government overreach when done by a Democrat.

Many policies have been proposed by Democrats that are talked about in the news, both for better or worse. But there is no counter-proposal from the Republican party. There is only a rejection of anything that is not tax cuts for the wealthiest Americans.

This does solidify a position they have held for decades, that the government does not work, which becomes a self-fulfilling prophecy. They get elected, do nothing, and say that the government does not do anything and should not be trusted.

The only major policy the Republican party has advanced has been tax cuts for the top 1% of individuals and raising them on everyone else to pay for them. This policy has been expanded upon by the last couple of Republican presidents, lowering the taxes on the wealthiest while raising them on the rest.

These same tax policies also encourage the wealthiest to participate in stock buybacks rather than building new factories or performing research and development. This just encourages the people who are making the most from the company's stock to get wealthy, while the people that make the company run, the workers, are left behind. We will talk more about this in later chapters.

If they wanted to, they could return to being a party of compassion, service, and personal responsibility. Many people who call themselves Republicans still see themselves this way, and frankly, many do share those traits. It is just that the political party itself no longer shares those values.

In recent memory, this party had Presidents Bush, who served in the military, showed compassion for the country, and did things that helped to bring people together. Additionally, the party had people like Senator McCain, who embodied all three of those traits.

Recently though, the party has moved away from any of those values. I also bet you think I will say it is one person's fault, but I am not because it is not just one person's fault. Life is complicated, and the cause of a problem is not always easy, nor is its solution.

There are good Republicans in leadership. But because of the toxicity, they are being vastly undercut. Liz Cheney was removed from Republican leadership for being honest about the election. Adam Kinzinger is retiring because of the toxicity within the party. Mitt Romney, the governor that enacted universal healthcare in Massachusetts and was the former presidential candidate, has been booed on stage. This is despite the fact that all of these people had voting records consistently on the right. Dan Crenshaw appears to be one of the few with integrity that his party hasn't undercut.

Conversely, people like Ted Cruz and Lindsay Graham used to be able, to tell the truth, despite any political inconvenience. Now they distort and lie so frequently that I am unsure why anyone pays attention to them.

Speaking of lies and what this party used to stand for, again, compassion, service, and personal responsibility, there is no finer example of how far the party has strayed than the January 6, 2021 insurrection at the U.S. Capitol building occurred. The people that took part in this event were lied to repeatedly by Republican party leaders and were told by right-leaning news outlets that the election was stolen.

What would you do if your leaders and the media repeatedly told you that the election was stolen? How upset would you be? What would you do?

This insurrection was led by people that had white-collar jobs, some of whom were business owners. This led to the realization of the extent to which people on the right had been lied to about everything and to the horrifying extent that had occurred. They had been lied to about the election, about who had won, and once they had been spun up so much that they led an insurrection, they were even lied to about the insurrection itself.

After the insurrection, right-leaning media and Republican party leaders again lied to the people about who was responsible for the violence and the damage. They lied to the point that a majority of them voted against an investigation into the insurrection. They knew that their lies would be uncovered. But they knew that their lies made them more popular.

These leaders within the Republican party did not show compassion to their constituents, who needed to understand that all because an election is lost, that hope is not. These leaders did not show responsibility for their actions. Instead, they hoped to blame everyone else. They definitely did not demonstrate service for their country as they encouraged an insurrection against it. These lies brought them political power, so they have continued using them.

It is these lies that made me rewrite large portions of this book. Those on the right are being lied to so much that they are conducting terrorist acts and leading an insurrection. Plus, they are lied to so much that they deny facts presented to them when they do not line up with the narrative they have been presented with. They have been told that the truth is a lie.

Originally when I first thought about writing this book, Bush was president. Even then, I saw the divisions that were happening. Back then, these divisions worried me too, but they were not as severe and nowhere near as violent. People could still talk to one another. They could still see the other as a fellow American, not an enemy. But now, we need to both focus on seeing each other as people while simultaneously focusing on solving issues. It is never too late, and we can do both.

Since we have been talking so much about lies, I want to define a couple of things that I think will help make things clear before we go further into this section. Let us start with the concept of gaslighting and how it applies to abusive relationships. Gas lighting is a form of psychological abuse that leads people to question the truth and what can be trusted. It leads people to question reality and leaves them with much anxiety. Also, the one doing the gaslighting convinces the victims that they are the only bastion of truth they can rely upon.

I have had this conversation with many friends and family over the years, and it never gets easier, but some of you are in an abusive relationship. You are in an abusive relationship with the Republican Party and its enablers. They are gaslighting you and twisting you into thinking that people that are different from you are coming to hurt you and that you have to take violent action to defend yourselves.

During Obama's administration, a lot was done to undermine his presidency. He was called illegal before he took office, and there was a massive effort to prove that he was illegitimate throughout his presidency. Unfortunately, these lies and many others made people believe that their only bastions of truth were the ones lying to them.

Here is the biggest problem. I know a lot of people on the right and Republicans. The vast majority of them are honest people with mountains of integrity. However, they are voting for people that are lying to them. They are voting for people who continue to manipulate them into not accepting reality.

As I mentioned earlier, most Republican politicians do not have mountains or even molehills of integrity. Liz Cheney was voted out of her leadership position for telling the truth about the 2020 election. They are not like their constituents, who pride themselves on their integrity and values.

Many of you so fiercely demand the integrity of our government that you tried starting the TEA (Taxed Enough Already) party. Later on, some were led into conducting an insurrection on the pretense of restoring integrity. Unfortunately, the anger from both of these was used to sharpen the lies and corruption instead of removing them. Remember the bridge to nowhere? For those who do not remember, an Alaskan senator added a rider to a bill to build a bridge to an island with a small number of residents. This ensured his vote for a bill at the time.

This practice was fairly standard but was also known as pork spending. It helped to get a lot of compromises accomplished but ended up causing a lot of random things to be put into federal law. Which a lot of people still do not like.

It was this practice that the TEA party stood up against and rallied behind to get them to quit. This was a good example of regular people stepping up and taking action to make change within the government. Preventing the government from getting too big and intrusive is a good thing.

However, the Republican party did not continue this trend of reform. Instead, they focused the anger of their constituents on ensuring that they could give away trillions of dollars to the wealthy while raising taxes on everyone else. Additionally, they allowed for additional loopholes which discouraged companies from investing in their employees or research. You do not like corruption. They only made it more corrupt.

You do not owe the Republican party anything. I know that many people seem to support the party because they are "your team," or they are not the Democratic Party. But that does not mean that they support you or your interests.

However, that's not good enough. You voted them into office. They work for you, not the other way around. They owe their loyalty to you; you do not owe it to them. It seems like this got lost somewhere along the line.

The current Republican party only wants you to serve them. They can not see anything larger than themselves. Hold the people that you nominate to a higher standard. Hold them up to at least the standard that you hold yourself.

To emphasize this, many of them have encouraged their constituents not to accept the 2020 election results and have decided instead to spin conspiracy theories about voter fraud and illegal ballots. To clarify, there is no proof of any election fraud significant enough to change the election's outcome.

Some politicians can not stand losing. They can not stand it so badly that they would rather destroy the foundations of our democracy and erode trust in the government than admit they lost. Think about that.

What would you do to your child if your kid lost a football game and behaved similarly? If your kid got so upset that he lost in the second half of the game that he wanted to destroy everything football related in your house and every store, he went to? What would you do? You would hold him responsible. You would remind him to be gracious in defeat. You would remind him that his self-worth is more than this one game.

For too long, the Republican party has appealed to the worst parts of our nature. They have been saying we need to fear poor, uneducated people fleeing violence in our country. They have said that we need to fear educational institutions. They have said that we need to fear the government. This has created a toxic environment where a country created by immigrants fears other immigrants, a place where we deride people who are educated, and where we think nothing good can come from working together.

To some extent, politicians of all types have been doing so forever. To be fair, these tactics are highly effective. These tactics allow politicians to stay in power by creating fear and division in those governed. They distract us from what they're doing, enabling them to do whatever they want without fear of repercussions because we are too busy fighting each other. We should be smart enough now to recognize these tactics and call them out.

But too many are letting the Republican party undermine our government and elections. We will discuss some specific examples throughout this book, but how about we address some of them now. There are far too many instances of the Republican party opposing legislation that most Americans support, including Republicans, just because they do not want to show a working government.

They are actively taking steps to suppress voting rights. To the point that when asked in front of the supreme court about these actions, they flat out said that if they do not suppress them, they will never win again.[1] That is not true.

Like I mentioned, the Republicans started agencies like the EPA. They worked hard to help bring the world together to fight other environmental catastrophes. There are ways that we can tackle the problems of today that hold onto those values. But we have to take the first step in admitting those problems exist.

Many people hold true to the values of what the Republican Party used to be. Frankly, I still think of myself as either an old-school Republican or a California Republican depending upon the context. You can value people, take care of the environment and still be pro-economic growth.

How about we jump back to the TEA party for a second. One good argument that I heard was that there are too many laws on the books and that we need to clean up our legal code. Despite the support this party got and the elections they won, these actions were never taken.

How many times are jokes made about the number of violations people commit just because there are outdated or conflicting laws on the books. It would have been nice to clean this up. But it never got done. Instead, politicians used this anger to get elected and then told you to be angry about something else. The reform and the changes you asked for never got done, started, or even seriously looked at for a change.

So, what is my ask of you? First, if a politician is trying to convince you to be afraid of something, take a step back and ask why. In many cases, it is to keep you distracted from what is happening and from holding them accountable.

Next, hold them responsible. If they are not being honest with their constituents, call them out. If they take a vacation to Mexico to avoid a winter storm that is destroying their state, hold them accountable. If they are not working on policies that improve the lives of their populace, call them out. If they support an insurrection of the capital, their place of work, call them out for not upholding their oaths to the constitution.

Conversely, don't jeer them if they are honest with the public. If a politician is honest, that needs to be encouraged, even if it is not the truth we want to hear. On the other hand, if they have not done anything their entire term, then challenge them in a primary election. Remember, they work for us, have to keep us happy, and are public servants.

Make the Republican party a legitimate party again. They have become a party focused on opposing any new legislation or making you afraid of what the Democrats are putting forward. The party's most popular members are currently focused on making splashy headlines or doing whatever they can for their own popularity, not on legislating or leading. Have them come up with ideas and legislation.

---

1. "In Supreme Court, Gop Attorney Defends Voting Restrictions by Saying They Help Republicans Win." NBCNews.com, NBCUniversal News Group, 3 Mar. 2021, https://www.nbcnews.com/politics/elections/supreme-court-gop-attorney-defends-voting-restrictions-saying-they-help-n1259305.

Chapter Five

The Democratic Party and the Politics of False Hope

Like the last section, let me start by saying I am talking about the Democratic party themselves, neither those on the left nor the right. There are members of the party that identify with both ends of the ideological spectrum. I know they get accused of only having members of the extreme left, but frankly, that is a joke. One of the reasons they have a hard time getting things done is because of the diversity of thought within the party and trying to make everyone happy.

As with the last section, this is about the Democratic party itself, the issues within it, specific topics, and the problems that need to be addressed within them will be addressed later. The Democratic party has a unique problem within U.S. politics. They have become a big tent party that includes everything from members of the right to the furthest left. Both authoritarians and libertarians.

This vast gulf in thought can make it difficult to accomplish anything within their own party, but that is not the problem I want to discuss. Instead, I want to talk about what they do to get in power compared to what they do when they get there.

There is a lot of work to be done in this country that has been laid bare in the past few years that needs to get fixed. Let me be clear, I said laid bare, as in exposed, not created, not caused. I'm sure that it would be nice to blame things on the previous president, but it is not his fault.

It would also be nice to say that these problems are caused by one "evil" group of people, but as I keep saying, and as I am sure life has shown you, this is rarely the case. With that in mind, there is no simple solution to our problems either.

Biden getting elected will not magically solve the problems facing our country. There is a lot of work that needs to be done if we continue working towards becoming that ideal shining city. Allowing the same deplorable policies under the Trump administration to continue under Biden undermines that goal.

The Democratic Party faces a different problem than the Republican party. Where the Republican party has a habit of lying to their constituents and sowing fear, the DNC has a habit of lying and providing false hope. A somewhat colorful example of this was when someone said that they voted Democrat instead of Republican because they knew they were going to get screwed over either way, but at least with the Democrats, they were getting kissed first.

While the Republican party is good at getting things accomplished, when they actually do something, the Democrats are stellar examples of snatching defeat from the jaws of victory. They can win both Legislative chambers and the Presidency and are unable to pass nearly universally popular legislation.

So, I said false hope, not actual hope, because hope has an underlying truth to it, the odds may be long, but there is still a chance for victory. The key is that you have to fight for it for there to be hope. False hope is built on a lie.

Why do I say that is true for the Democrats? Because every time a politician is willing to implement real structural change, work across the aisle, and actually make policies that improve people's lives, they are undermined and sidelined by the larger political party. This behavior was also illustrated in the above discussion about the Republican party.

The Democratic party is surprisingly good at this because several extremely effective and popular Democrats have been sidelined to maintain the status quo. While the RNC encourages its politicians to lie, the Democratic party encourages its politicians to maintain a status quo that actively harms people. It is like they are proud of the moniker of "do-nothing Democrats."

For a 'fun' example of the Democratic party undermining and sidelining their own effective politicians, let's look at Representative Katie Porter. Of course, I could have picked plenty of other politicians, some of which are famous for being sidelined, but instead of providing an overwhelming list of examples, I thought I would just focus on one.

For those that do not know, she served on the Financial Services Committee and was well known for asking very tough and pointed questions. She is also well known for bringing in a whiteboard to have the people testifying before the committee to show the math. Which I believe the average citizen would prefer if they were watching someone testify before a House Committee. However, the Democrats chastised her repeatedly for asking tough questions and holding people accountable. So much so that she was removed from the committee.

She is not the only person like this. She worked hard and did her job, and instead of being praised for it because of the results she was getting, they decided to sideline her. She did what she was elected to do, and the Democratic leadership did not like it, so they stopped her. The Democratic party leadership has a terrible history of doing this recently.

In fact, how about we look at the Democratic Party in Nevada. First off, as a quick primer, there are lots and lots of progressive policies that are popular with the majority of the country. Progressives have crazy ideas like getting the government to work for the people instead of the other way around. Which is one reason they are so popular. Progressives also tend to run for office on the Democratic party ticket.

Going back to Nevada, progressives won the leadership of the Nevada Democratic Party, which led all other party officials to resign but not before giving away a lot of the party's money. With that in mind, every time a progressive starts to make inroads in politics, the establishment Democrats go out of their way to undermine them.

How about we look at the most recent cycle of presidential elections. Many promises were made during this cycle to do things like raise the minimum wage or work on infrastructure that seems to be forgotten when it comes to implementing political change. Granted, Biden is not the first president to talk a big game about fixing our nation's problems. Trump and Obama did too, and I think you get the idea.

The main motivator that helped to elect Trump was the anger and frustration that the general population had with "politics as usual" in Washington. Why do I bring this up here? Because the Democratic party went out of their way, two presidential elections in a row, to ensure that an establishment person won the party's nomination rather than the enormously popular person that would have changed things to improve people's lives.

The Democratic party would have rather lost to Trump and did once than fundamentally change the system. They actively do not want to change the system and will undermine people that try to do so. This makes their promises a false hope.

One thing I talked about with some of my right-leaning friends before the election is why they seemed so scared of Biden? They said they feared the very leftist policies that he expressed. The problem is that he only took moderate positions to appease the left while not alienating the right.

But since the Democratic party is the only one willing to listen to the left, I could see the confusion and how the signals got twisted. Biden was one of the senators that passed the crime bill in the 1990s where Hillary Clinton called black people "Super predators," like they were cartoonish science fiction villains. He was not, and is not, a left-leaning politician. Since being elected, Biden has also not done many things he promised to do to help repressed communities.

In fact, there are a lot of policies that Trump had in place that Biden has allowed to remain. Do you remember getting upset about Trump breaking the nuclear deal with Iran? Are you still upset with Biden about leaving it broken? Were you upset about the child separation at the border under Trump? Are you upset about it under Biden? Same policies, different sales tactics. Why do you allow it under one administration if you did not like it under another?

We can be upset that both Trump[1] and Biden[2] abandoned U.S. allies, allowed our enemies to regain strongholds, and acquired lots of U.S. equipment left behind. We should expect better of our elected officials. These two are far more similar than many people are willing to admit.

So, while I say to my right-leaning readers, do not be scared, I doubt he will do anything, let alone the things you are worried about. Frankly, for you, that is my ask for this section; you get off easy here.

To my left-leaning readers, I want you to realize that other than toning down the rhetoric, he probably will not do much to help the country heal, which is a problem. A problem for all of us because while Trump exacerbated and highlighted some problems, I do not think Biden will fix them.

Therefore, my ask for my left-leaning readers is going to be different. I want you to be more like my right-leaning readers, get a plan and focus on it. Pay attention to local politics. Get involved at a local level. Support the politicians that are doing something to improve your communities. Because the DNC's plan is very similar to that of the RNC, stay in power.

Regarding earlier topics like abortion and gun reform, those on the right have a fairly simple plan: "no." But at least they have a plan, and they stay on message. But when it comes to topics like abortion, those on the left are relying upon court cases that are decades old instead of enshrining women's autonomy into legislative action. Even in 2022, the Democratic Party worked to ensure that a candidate that believed in a woman's autonomy lost to a candidate that didn't.

An example of the messaging problem is that Biden, a man that has been a lifelong churchgoer and man of (a historically very conservative) faith is not as popular amongst religious conservatives in the U.S. as a man that never goes to church, does not know anything about the bible, gassed people in front of a church so he could hold a bible upside down for a photo op, and had his followers worship a literal golden idol of him.

Lastly, I will ask the same about Democrats that I asked those who continue to vote Republican. Hold them accountable. They are public servants that serve you. Our society changes and our government should not be stagnant around it. Our constitution is a living document, hence the amendments.

The status quo only works for a surprisingly short amount of time and a very small amount of people. If our politicians do not represent us, they need to be challenged in the primary elections. Term limits for legislators have been enormously popular across the political spectrum for over 40 years, but nothing has ever happened to implement them. We can help to change that. Get legislators that represent your community, not some ideological or political purity test.

---

1. Robert Burns, Lolita C. Baldor. "Trump Defends Decision to Abandon Kurdish Allies in Syria." AP NEWS, Associated Press, 8 Oct. 2019, https://apnews.com/article/donald-trump-syria-ap-top-news-international-news-politics-ac3115b4eb564288a03a5b8be868d2e5.
2. Brennan , David, et al. "Joe Biden Abandoned Us, Say Afghan Politicians as Taliban Forms Government." Newsweek, 3 Sept. 2021, https://www.newsweek.com/joe-biden-abandoned-us-afghan-politicians-taliban-forms-government-omar-zakhilwal-azra-jafari-1625729.

Chapter Six

Traditional Media, Manipulation, and the Need to Diversify

Here is one section that I want you to take a lot from because this section is about the networks actively working to divide us the most. Many aspects of our modern media actively work against our best interests. Additionally, they are the ones that intentionally go out of the way to make sure that we do not see each other as fully developed human beings. Because fear sells, and getting us afraid of our neighbors keeps us tuned into them.

How many times has the media described the other side of the political spectrum as uneducated or filled with hate towards the country? How many times has the media told us that the other side is destroying this country? Please note that I did not clarify which media outlet because far too many members of the media convey that message. However, I would be remiss if I did not note that one outlet has damaged it far worse.

All of us, myself included, have been manipulated into thinking that those we don't agree with are violent and are actively seeking to destroy this country. It is very easy to get trapped within a self-reinforcing bubble of media input, and it is hard to recognize when this happens, making it even harder to come out of these media bubbles.

But we all have to do this because only then will we be able to see the humanity in one another and collaborate to get things done. To be fair, keeping us in these media bubbles keeps us watching, preventing us from working together, intentionally, or unintentionally. Imagine what we could accomplish if we did. It would be fantastic to find out.

Like most of the problems I will be writing about, this will only pertain to the media in the U.S.; however, this is not solely a U.S. problem. In fact, it is easily argued that the problem is worse in other countries. Because of our First Amendment, the government has no say in what a news or "news" agency can report. Therefore, these agencies have a tremendous amount of leeway in what they are allowed to report.

This is not true in the rest of the world, even if you exclude countries that only allow state-run propaganda in the place of news or think that "reeducation camps" are a viable method to ensure the populace doesn't challenge the approved government message. Even in the Western world, countries such as Britain and Australia have taken strides to control what the press is allowed to report and how they are allowed to frame certain reporting.

This means that even though I will disparage a lot of U.S. media, one outlet in particular, I will only encourage us, the consumers of that media, to take action, not the government in any way because I would rather deal with the problems we have than exacerbate them.

Having freedom is hard. It puts a lot of responsibility on the people. But this freedom allows us to have a media that works for us, holding the government responsible, rather than one that undermines us and misleads us,

Before we talk about media bias, we should talk about bias in general. Everyone has a bias; this is just leaning towards one side or another on a topic. There is nothing inherently wrong with this behavior.

The key is recognizing your bias and adjusting your inputs accordingly. It's hard to do this, as when something confirms our bias, we feel validated and, therefore, good. It feels comfortable.

But staying solely within a media environment that never challenges your beliefs can become dangerous. It crosses this threshold when your bias prevents you from seeing reality or others as less than human and can lead to dangerous behavior. This level of comfort can prevent us from seeing anything from someone else's perspective.

This easy level of comfort is also dangerous when we only enjoy things that reflect our own bias. In today's environment of 24-hour news networks and cultivated social media feeds, which we will discuss later, it is far too easy for us to create a bubble of information that actively rejects disparate information. This is where many of us are and where we need to come back from. We need to leave our comfortable media bubbles and start seeing things from other perspectives.

Now let us talk about bias in the media. Again, this is not inherently a bad thing; however, this does become a problem when people can no longer agree on reality. Having a liberal or conservative opinion on responding to an event is one thing, but distorting reality to say the event never happened is completely different.

The media's biggest bias over a liberal or conservative slant is the desire to sensationalize. This means that they may run a breaking story, but not all the facts are available. They do this because it makes a great headline, which brings views and makes them money. However, once all of the facts are in the story may not be as exciting or interesting, or they were completely wrong about the subject, so while the story may get reported, it will be downplayed.

This bias towards sensationalism makes sense and has always been true. News outlets need to make money. But that leaves the onus on us to be smart consumers of this information. So let us get started.

How often have we been told that liberals, or conservatives, are going to destroy this country? How often has the media shown images that confirm this opinion? But what about the facts that don't conform with the presented narrative?

For example, how often have you been shown a negative picture of a president? But aren't all of the pictures about the president that you always like positive? If that's the message you're getting from your media, you are missing an entire side of the story.

What happens when you talk to someone you disagree with on the other side? Once they are humanized, do they still seem like an enemy? Probably not, but our media is not helping us see one another.

One thing we can do is look at the bias of the information we receive. There are many resources available to see how biased your new media is, both in terms of the liberal and conservative slant that we have been primarily talking about and whether or not they are primarily concerned with presenting the facts or are just an opinion.

Both of these biases have a major impact on the type of information that we receive. Having a news show that only provides facts that support one side or another is fairly damaging. Because then we only see one side of an argument, not the other. This makes us think that the facts are always on our side when they may not be.

Compounding this problem is that most popular segments on news channels are their opinion shows, which, by definition, do not have to provide facts. Therefore, if people are just paying attention to opinion pieces, they are most likely not getting any factual information and have a distorted view of the world.

Let us take the Fox News channel as an example. Looking at the detailed media bias charts, they are further to the right than an agency like the MSNBC channel is to the left. This makes sense because Fox started with the intent to be a right-leaning news organization, as their viewers know.

Here is the thing, I am picking the Fox channel for a couple of reasons. First, they are currently in the middle of several lawsuits for providing false information and manipulating the public. Second, people who watch Fox, or other outlets with a very overt bias, know what they are doing, and Fox is the most popular. Before anyone thinks this is limited to Fox, the left also has media companies that provide similar levels of bias. Lastly, please note that I am talking about their tv channel, not their website, which rates higher on providing factual news coverage.

But before we go down this specific rabbit hole, let's talk about the people that watch Fox News. They know that it has a bias. In fact, that's one of the reasons that they went to that outlet. Because before Fox came along, a significant portion of the population did not see themselves represented in the media.

Plus, they felt like the slant being presented to them in other media outlets continually cast them and conservative opinions in a negative light. This left them yearning for information, which is understandable. However, if no media presented your ideas and views in a positive light, you would seek out media that does, which leads us into a spiral we will discuss later.

For now, that's why I am not going to argue that viewers of Fox turn to outlets like CNN or MSNBC. That's also why I will ask that people that watch Fox are not looked down upon because the attitude of exclusion and elitism drove them to Fox in the first place. It also reinforces the behavior that they are not free to discuss their ideas.

To begin with, Rupert Murdoch said that he started Fox as a conservative outlet. They slant heavily towards the opinion side of the house and away from factual information. But that is also why people tune into the network. Their opinion shows have traditionally brought them the most viewers.

Ironically, these opinion shows have led to the most trouble for the network, bringing them multiple lawsuits. Additionally, in court cases, they have stated that no rational person would believe what their very popular on-air personalities have said and have lost numerous court cases when their lies and distortions have gone too far. Which, for those that do watch Fox, is why I strongly encourage them to get their news from other outlets. If they want to continue to watch it for the drama and entertainment, they should do so with the knowledge that they are not providing them with facts.

Here is another reason I chose Fox and ties back to the larger point about media bubbles. When Fox was accused of not being far enough on the right by their viewers, and they were challenging the bubble of information they had formed, people started to tune them out. This also allowed other outlets that were even further to the right to grow in popularity.

These people wanted confirmation of the information within their bubble. Which further distorted the level of disinformation that was happening in the country. People did not want their beliefs challenged, so to keep them, they went further to the right, which amplified those ideas.

This generated a problem where they could no longer be swayed by facts to get them out of their bubble. Because instead of focusing on facts and then doing a conservative analysis, their media removed the facts from their audience. For example, climate change, which we will discuss later, is a problem. However, instead of arguing for market-based solutions, i.e., a conservative solution, they said it isn't happening.

Or more immediately, despite having strict vaccine and mask requirements within those media outlets, they continued to doubt their effectiveness and encouraged their viewers not to comply. So once they tried to start reintroducing facts to the conversation, that wasn't what their audience was used to hearing, nor did they want to hear it, so they tuned out, thinking that Fox had become part of the elite media.

The last reason I chose Fox, which only applies to the media on the right, is that they say they are the only source of reliable information. They promote the ideas of fake news, and those other media outlets are mainstream while unironically bragging about having the largest viewership. Now there is nothing inherently wrong with a conservative slant to the news. My only complaint about on-screen reporters like Chris Wallace is that there are too few like him.

Too often, media outlets, like Fox, tend to hire 'personalities' rather than reporters. This means that they are saying, either explicitly or under the guise of "asking questions, " how the left is coming to take your guns, shrink your home values, and destroy the country's moral fabric. There are many valid criticisms of liberals and Democrats, but tan suits and selfie sticks should not be among them.

Now I've been picking on Fox, but here is a lesson for all of us. I encourage all of us to diversify our media sources, especially if the media proclaims that those who disagree with you are the enemies of this country. If the media is saying that everyone who disagrees with you hates this country, then you need a new media outlet.

Those on the left and right have served shoulder to shoulder on the literal front lines of combat, to the metaphorical front lines of dealing with some of the worst social issues we face. They stand together. You have stood with these people, whether you know it or not. They are not the enemy. If the media you consume tells you so, you need to change the channel.

Because if that does not happen, we believe that an election is stolen, and storming the capital is an appropriate response. I wish that were a euphemism or an exaggeration. But there were so many people in the media questioning the election's legitimacy that regular people felt they had no choice but to storm the capital.

For those who knew the election wasn't stolen, how would you feel if your media sources repeatedly told you that the election was stolen? What would you think? If politicians and the media repeatedly told you that the election was stolen, then it logically makes sense to take action against that.

However, here is the problem, which we will discuss again later in the section on voting. There was zero evidence that it was stolen. There was zero evidence that there were any problems with the election. Yet political figures like Trump, Cruz, and Hawley, did not allow a lack of evidence to prevent them from making claims that there were problems with the election. Conservative media outlets saw that a stolen election would make a huge story, so they ran with it. Again, all of this is without evidence.

Therefore, everyone that took part in the insurrection had all of their elected leaders and media telling them for months that the election was stolen. It did not matter that they did not present evidence; even in a courtroom, everyone they trusted was telling them the same thing. So, they took action.

Conversely, as we discussed previously, once Biden was in office, many of the policies people were upset about under Trump were no longer covered. These policies didn't change, but the level and type of reporting did. This leads to the complaint from the right that the media was biased against Trump to play out, in real-time, as very accurate.

This goes back to the reason people turned to networks like Fox in the first place. Speaking of which, another conservative talking point about the media, that they secretly loved Trump, may also be true. Lots of the fear-mongering went down after the election, as well as the ratings for most major news outlets, Fox included.

This is why I say to diversify your media consumption, don't just listen to one side or only those who agree with you. There are examples of times when I have gotten caught up in my media, unaware of some things that have taken place. Fortunately, I have had friends who help keep me from insulating myself in a media bubble.

Also, if you are going to look at the news, look beyond the front page. The splashy headlines are meant to grab our attention, but they do not tell the entire story. Find smaller independent journalists. Look for local news when there is an issue. One great thing is we can find the local news anywhere, and they always have a person there covering what is happening.

Local news sources are one source that I highly recommend we all incorporate into our media feeds. First off, these sources cover news that directly impacts our communities, and in turn, they are the sources that we can greatly impact. Additionally, our local channels and papers would really appreciate the attention. There are lots of local news organizations that need financial assistance.

In too many cases, local news outlets are either being bought by large companies to make them homogeneous or by hedge funds selling off all of their assets. This reduces the quality of information that we receive from these local outlets. So not only should we pay more attention to these news sources to protect ourselves, we need to do so to protect them.

One more thing, think about how many former politicians are on major media outlets. Sure, some of them are helpful to give political analysis, but many are there to help members of their party get elected and denounce the other party, no matter what is being said.

This change in the media can come about by voting with your wallet. If you give viewership to a company that advocates for the death of those that oppose you or states that people that disagree with you want to kill you, again, I wish that was a euphemism, then change the channel. These companies care about viewership because this equals money. We can change what media we are ingesting.

Lastly, while I was pointing out a lot of the problems with Fox, notice that I didn't call them fake news. If we live in a society with an open press, we have to accept that and all that it stands for, which means hearing things that we may not agree with.

Therefore, I would ask that if someone calls an outlet, or series of outlets, "fake news," then don't take that person seriously. They are trying to suppress viewpoints, and this has even led to violence. Calling the media "fake news" is a tactic of dictators, and when that behavior was brought into our political lexicon, even more, authoritarian governments felt comfortable calling the media "fake news."

Chapter Seven

Social Media and Maintaining Your Bubble

Now that we have discussed more traditional media let's focus on social media. This has enabled us to be closer to those distant from us, but it has also enabled us to insulate ourselves into thought bubbles. While this is the nature of the outlets, we have to, like with traditional media, be smart consumers.

First off, social media has done a lot of wonderful things. We can stay connected to the people that have come into our lives and left a lasting impact. This means that we can continue to enjoy their company despite the distance. This interconnectivity allows us to spread information very quickly; however, this also allows misinformation to spread quickly.

Some of this misinformation is that people on the left do not have jobs and want everything for free, and those on the right are uneducated fascists. It's easy to believe in these stereotypes and come up with a caricature of those that disagree with you. But mindful, thoughtful people can disagree on a subject.

Let's start by discussing an inherent issue with social media. Primarily, when they were first created, we, as consumers, said that we did not want to pay for these social media platforms or much of the internet. This placed these companies in a position where they needed to create a revenue stream to provide the expected services.

As expected, they turned to generate revenue through the use of advertising. But now, they had access to something no advertising agency had ever had. Us. All of us, and all of our information. We gave it to them.

This allowed these companies to make money by mining our data to find out who we are and what we like and therefore target advertisements specifically to whatever we may need or find interesting. Another way to look at this is that if you are not paying for a service, you are the product, and that is what social media has become; we are the products being sold.

Another way of putting it is that these companies thrive off of engagement. That means they look at what we like and where we leave comments. This ensures that we stay on their sites for as long as possible, providing them with more data and allowing them to sell us more goods and services.

This behavior is not an inherently bad thing. We collectively agreed that we didn't want to pay for these services. They needed to make money, and we provided them with all our information. This leads directly to the problem social media creates within our society.

For now, though, we have established that these companies know what you like and what interests you, making it really simple for them to target you with similar goods and services. While we can find this beneficial for Google or Facebook to see that we are interested in a specific subject, we can therefore recommend a product or service tailored to that desire.

Unfortunately, this same process can become harmful when these sites encourage us to only associate with people with the same ideologies. This engagement can take us down rabbit holes that alienate us from people we may disagree with and then convince us that they are our enemies. It is a very slippery slope; if it does not happen regularly, it could be dismissed.

This brings my first ask to us for this section: first, define for ourselves what we want our social media feeds to accomplish. This can be hard to do and harder to stick with. Pay attention to what is in our feeds. Radicalization happens slowly; if you notice that the media is leading you down that path, change direction. Keep those feeds hidden.

An issue that stems from this and is becoming pervasive on social media is that many people are culling their friend's lists of people they disagree with. Let us be fair, though. These past few years have been very difficult for all of us. It has limited or removed us from being able to interact with people face to face, which has forced us to take these conversations online, which can be far more difficult. There are conversations that I have had in real life that worked very well, but when I tried to have similar conversations with the same people online, they fell flat and did not work.

However, that does not mean we should not try. One thing to remember when talking with friends you disagree with is to recognize the friendship throughout. We can talk about things that unite us while discussing our disagreements. The point here is that our online selves are not who we are in the real world, and we need to recognize the humanity in one another while having these conversations.

We have probably all heard that these conversations through social media do not work to change people's minds. But these platforms have become a great way to disseminate a lot of information to our friends and family. So, what is the compromise, then?

Well, think about what you want from the platform you are using. Then, think about the platform itself and what it can provide to you. Do you wish to have a place where you can share family pictures? Do you want to plan events? Do you want to connect with friends and family you are physically distant from? Do you want to learn a new skill? Do you want to share your political view and then cut out anyone that disagrees with you? Do you just want to watch cat videos?

Speaking of sharing ideas on social media, it is very unfortunate to see when people have culled their lists of people that do not agree with them and then ask a question meant for people that do not agree with them. This behavior then reinforces itself by stating that when there is no reply to these comments, those who disagree must be cowards or have no defense for these actions.

It does not occur to anyone that those that may disagree with them or have an opinion on the matter have been removed from their friend's list. Or that the environment is now so toxic that they no longer want to engage. When we create a thought bubble that only allows one thought inside, do not be surprised when there is no dissent. I'm sure many of us have seen this occur in our feeds.

I know it is much easier to read our feeds when there are no dissenting thoughts. We are not challenged, and no one is learning. Plus, this allows us to become radicalized because if you engage with this topic, you may want to engage further without a dissenting opinion.

Plus, if we keep trimming our feeds, we will miss a lot of information. We will miss when friends are in pain or need help, just because we disagree with them on a topic or how to handle it. I know that I have learned a lot by keeping my feed open to both sides.

I have learned a lot about the pain experienced by people I had no idea was occurring. I have also had to walk away from my social media occasionally because of the toxicity. I have even been able to help people see when they've gone too far down a path, but only when talking to them in person.

We need to try not to limit ourselves to voices or topics that we want to hear or agree with our opinion. This will prevent us from hearing limited messaging that makes it impossible for us to see another point of view.

Lastly, when we disagree with someone, we could take it offline or do it through direct messaging. That will help us continue to see the humanity in one another and remember that we are still friends. After all, we did make friends with this person for some reason. So try to remember that when we disagree.

Chapter Eight

Owning Your Power

Before we move on to the next chapter, I would like to reiterate the main point of this section. We have more power than we know.

People want to limit our voices by limiting our choices. Our government officials highly value our votes and want to use us to increase their political power. But we must remember that they serve us and our power, not theirs. Political parties use segments of our population as a voting block, and we need to hold them accountable so that they no longer see us as a tool to manipulate.

Traditional and social media recognize that our attention and information are worth trillions of dollars. That alone gives us tremendous power. That is why those that disagree with us are painted in such an unfavorable light, and those that agree with us are infallible. A friend of mine said that he turns off his media if he finds that either he is yelling at it or it is yelling at him. This is a good lesson.

The rest of this book deals with specific topics that we disagree on, and in many of those sections, I will attempt to get us to see a perspective we may not have had before. Regardless, I want you to know that we can have these conversations. Some of which are very difficult or painful.

In each of the following sections, there are points where we can work together. We can work to understand one another, even if we don't agree. We can own our collective power to fix the problems that we have in our society, or at the very least not let them further divide us.

Chapter Nine

Dividing Lines and Commonality

This section of the book is designed for differences of opinion that we have on certain topics. There are strong and valid points of contention here, but there is more common ground on these subjects than things that divide us. However, these disagreements are usually exploited to make it seem like we are divided and cannot have an honest conversation about these problems. This exploitation of differences allows people to have power over us. Because if we work together on these issues, we could solve them in a way that addresses all our concerns and address the things that are truly harming our society.

That doesn't mean that the issues addressed in this section aren't problems; it just means that there is more uniting than dividing us. This section will look at some of the issues we must face in our country. Many of these are issues that we all agree are broken, and there are many diverse ideas on how to solve them, most of which are not mutually exclusive. It is possible that we can work together to come up with a better solution and solve many of the problems we are facing. We are not each other's enemy.

This section will start by looking at what it means to be responsible and held accountable for one's actions. Then we will move on to topics everyone loves to talk about, taxes, and how we can ensure that we have more money in our pockets at the end of the day. Additionally, we will be talking about our educational and prison systems and how we handle gun rights and policing. For each of these topics, those on the left and right make good points. Most of which have been drowned out by our respective media channels and social media feeds.

Like the book's previous section, I will make a call to action for all of us. For a while, it is easy to point out the problems; it is harder to fix them. But like many of these problems, there was a concerted effort to put them in place as well as some of them have been around for decades, making it seem like they are the way they have always been. But that is not always the case, and we can always take responsibility and fix past errors. Especially working together.

Chapter Ten

Freedom and Responsibility

Let's start by talking about freedom and responsibility. Looking at how many people in our society are behaving, it is very apparent that people use their freedom to deny their responsibilities and repress other people's freedoms. Many of us still know that taking care of our responsibilities ends up giving us more freedom in the long term. Neglecting those responsibilities always ends up chaining us.

Too many people have begun to view their personal freedom as paramount without considering how it affects others. It is their freedom at the expense of everyone else's. This is a selfish and destructive way of thinking. Our freedoms end when it takes away other people's freedom. Our government should help to define those boundaries with laws. Some of them are creating laws that help define those boundaries; others are actively working to confuse the matter and bring out the worst in us.

Should anyone be able to come into our home without permission? No. I think we all understand that. But what boundaries should exist when we interact with other members of society.

Let's talk about how we treated the people we claim were "essential" workers during the pandemic. Specifically, hospital workers, those that kept stores open, and warehouse workers. Basically, these people allowed us to maintain our lives while locked down or cared for us when we were sick.

How many times were doctors and nurses yelled at for begging people to care for their fellow citizens? How many times were they accused of being part of a grand conspiracy? These medical professionals have sworn to care for us. They swore to 'do no harm,' yet people thought the worst of them. They were, and are still, acting in a way responsible to their oaths and society at large.

This social responsibility limited their own freedom. That was their choice. However, their freedom is still being limited by people who are being irresponsible, ironically in the name of freedom. That was the choice of those unwilling to care for their health, limiting the freedoms of those medical professionals. These caregivers are having their freedoms removed because people are being irresponsible.

When store clerks or warehouse workers ensured that we received as many supplies as we needed or wanted during the pandemic, we praised them. We held them up as being essential. However, when they started to unionize and demand better pay and treatment, some claimed that they were being selfish. Ensuring they have better pay and benefits would ensure they had greater freedom in their lives.

We used to have a better understanding of this communal responsibility. For example, during wartime, there used to be efforts to limit consumption, start "Liberty gardens," and contribute to the war effort in various ways. We used to understand that temporarily limiting our own freedoms and taking responsibility for our greater communities had ensured our freedom instead of removing it.

Unfortunately, these kinds of efforts also used to be led by the government. The government used to ask us to make sacrifices to ensure our freedoms, and we would step up to that responsibility. Now, government officials cast doubt upon infectious disease experts to ensure that we do not have to take any form of responsibility. Or they tell us that in times of crisis, we shouldn't make sacrifices; we should just go shopping.

Or, in some cases, politicians will prioritize an individual's freedom at the expense of all responsibility that person may have to their community or fellow citizens. For example, stand your ground laws can make sense. For those that may be unaware, these laws state that there is no obligation to back down from a dangerous situation if you are allowed to be in a location, the best example is your home, but this applies to public areas as well.

Now, these laws can make sense if enforced correctly. These laws can ensure that you are taking responsibility for your safety and not allowing others to limit your freedoms. Because, as we will talk about later, your safety is ultimately your responsibility.

Unfortunately, the line of thinking that we are allowed to murder anyone we feel threatened by legally is easy to corrupt, especially if it goes from allowing you to responsibly protect yourself from harm to exerting your freedoms on others, as it has been. Recent examples of laws allowing this type of behavior include Florida granting the authority to its citizens to run over protestors because they are being inconvenienced and Texas was allowing bounties to be taken out on women and anyone associated with them who are seeking healthcare.

Just like us, government functions best when it enables us to behave responsibly. Our government functions at its worst when it limits its citizens' freedoms. It's a tightrope to walk, but it's one that we have done in many cases and are perfectly capable of doing.

My next ask for this section is fairly simple. Basically, it's the Golden Rule: Do unto others as you would have them do unto you. Remember that taking responsibility for our actions does not limit our freedoms; it enables them to endure long term. Right now, the discussion provides a great example, but it is a theme that will constantly be addressed. Many people are being encouraged to behave irresponsibly, primarily hurting themselves and denying themselves the freedom of living.

Next is to hold ourselves and our government responsible; after all, we are a government of the people. Our politicians work for us, and many of them seek to deny our freedoms and responsibilities, all while shouting "freedom." We need to hold them to the task. If they pass laws that allow us to hurt one another or specifically target a group of people, we need to remove those laws and those politicians. We need to support one another when we protest oppression.

Chapter Eleven

Cancelling Cancel Culture, Keeping Consequence Culture

Speaking of responsibility, how about we get rid of "cancel culture"? I bet many of us would be in favor of getting rid of that, but what does that mean? We all seem to agree that this culture is not productive and adds toxicity to any opportunity for people to grow and change. Plus, it allows people to feel like they are being responsible for "cancelling" someone or something without doing any actual work or growth on their own.

However, we should keep and expand upon "consequence culture." Cancel culture started as an attempt to hold people responsible for their actions. But it turned into a shorthand way of trying to dismiss people without actually holding them accountable. It may feel good for a group of people to go online and say that they have "cancelled" someone for doing something wrong, but a few steps are missing.

First, this "cancelling" can happen before there's been any verification or understanding that something negative happened. Or that it happens so fast that there is no time for the person being "cancelled" even to know that they have done something inappropriate. This prevents an understanding of the problem but allows rage to focus on a target.

Since this can happen so fast, it can also prevent accountability for legitimate crimes by allowing the perpetrator to paint themselves as the victim. Or it can conversely demonize a person for simply misspeaking. Neither of these scenarios is holding a person accountable.

Fundamentally there is a difference between holding someone accountable and what has become a "cancel" culture. If someone legitimately does something wrong, this needs to be brought to light so that the perpetrators can be held accountable and victims can go through the healing process. However, should someone lose everything in their lives because they made a statement, sometimes ill-informed, sometimes just not funny?

Most of us think that people should be held responsible for their actions. This is something that most of us can agree upon. However, if we get caught up in only looking at the other side of the political spectrum while excusing those we may agree with, that is a problem. Being held responsible for one's actions should not depend on which side of the spectrum one holds.

For example, many politicians have committed sexual harassment or assault in both political parties. However, each political party seems to excuse the behavior of its own members. Additionally, depending on the media we consume, we may never hear that this behavior is taking place.

Many people knew about former governor Andrew Cuomo's behavior before he was removed from office. But that story, while known to some, was kept out of larger media outlets. The mass exodus of female talent from Fox News due to sexual harassment and assault isn't covered on their network. Many of the responsible parties in these stories are neither being "cancelled" nor held responsible.

Plenty of powerful people get away with crimes that need to be held accountable. Our political parties and media always want us to think about the criminal behavior of those on the opposite party but to excuse the criminal behavior of those they align with. We should not allow this to happen, which is why I brought up the need to diversify our media inputs. We need to hold all of these people accountable.

Let's take a moment and go back to the reasons to cancel "cancel" culture. As a movement, it prevents people from the opportunity to change and grow. There are many things in life that we will never experience and can only learn from others. That is, we will all say or do the "wrong thing" from time to time, but should we hold someone permanently responsible for something they naively said?

If someone makes a misstep, says something out of ignorance, or is a product of their times (i.e., cancelling someone from history), what is the point of cancelling them? Are we just trying to make ourselves feel good? Are we trying to say that we did something and that we took action by helping to cancel someone? Is that really making the world better? Is that affecting the change that we want to see? Did anyone learn anything?

Picture this, someone has been recruited into a Nazi group, and their social media feeds become filled with hate speech. However, now they realize they want to change; they no longer want to be filled with hate. So now they have come out and are no longer in this hate group. Should the hate speech they said always follow them around? Should they be denied jobs, friends, and housing because they once said something hateful? Are they not allowed to grow? Are they not allowed to reenter society?

Notice that while I said their speech was filled with hate, they did not actually commit a crime. There are lots of people in society that at one point thought or said something horrible. They should be allowed to grow and heal. They should be allowed to learn. They should be allowed to change.

This is particularly relevant because so much of our lives are led online and visible to so many people. This means that if someone currently expresses beliefs that hurt other people, it is easier for that to gain a lot of visibility. But if we ever expect them to grow within our society, we have to give them the room to make mistakes and learn without ostracizing them.

Think about the things that we have all posted on your media feeds. Think about the fact that they never go away (a concern that my kids will have to live with more than my generation or my parents). Now think about being held accountable for an opinion you had a decade ago. Do you still have that opinion? Did you change your mind? Should you still be held accountable for that opinion? Should you still be held to the standard of that opinion? Or are you allowed to grow? Are you allowed to change your mind?

Our society has been changing a lot in the last few decades, which I will get to numerous times through this book, and that has scared and confused some people, and I think that is understandable. It can be confusing if you shake up a society and change norms. We need to give people the space to catch up. Some people don't see that these changes are about respecting one another. Some see these changes as an erosion of power.

Conversely, if you are one of those people for whom the world is changing around you, and you feel a little afraid and out of touch. Don't worry; you are not alone. You will make mistakes, but that is okay. We are all human. Have patience with yourself and have patience with others. People just want respect and to be recognized for who they are. Plus, as I will discuss in various sections, things aren't changing as much as we think.

Lastly, we need to remove the "cancel" culture because it is being used as a weapon to divide us and sow fear amongst us. We are being told things like there is a war on Christmas, on marriage, or history. These lies make people feel oppressed and attacked so they can stand behind certain politicians or watch certain media outlets.

Actions like removing statues of traitors to the U.S. government do not cancel history. Teaching that slavery was bad is not cancelling history. Burning books and banning them from libraries is an attempt to cancel history and prevent people from learning about it. Plus, if we never learn about the atrocities of previous generations, we can not hold our current politicians responsible when they start to take similar actions.

With that in mind, my first request is that people be allowed to make mistakes. If no crime was committed, then use it as an opportunity to teach one another. We can't all possibly know everything, so we should allow for mistakes to happen without ruining someone's life. Besides, no good comes from that.

We should show others the same compassion that we would like them to show us. Yes, I just paraphrased the Golden Rule. If we want to make the world a better place, we must allow people to grow and change. Part of that process is making mistakes. We all do that, and we should be allowed to do better.

The second thing is to hold people accountable for their actions. This is harder than the previous one because while that can be done with a tweet, this ask takes reflection and work. Plus, there will be people you agree with who need to be held accountable for the harm they have caused. When this happens to someone you agree with, I will encourage you to think of this as a win for justice, not a loss for your "team."

If your media feeds or politicians say something has been "cancelled," I will encourage you to diversify and try to get another perspective. In many cases, if your media is making those that disagree with you out to be evil, it's probably time to switch it up. Lastly, there are far more dangerous examples of "cancelling" people and things, but we will discuss that further in the book.

Chapter Twelve

Equality of Opportunity through Education

There are quite a few problems with our perceptions and expectations of our educational system, most of which I will not be covering, but I will try to highlight some here. First, the education we receive until our high school graduation is undervalued, under-resourced, and over-tested. Next, while our institutions of higher learning are among the best in the world, they are becoming inaccessible to most of us because of the oppressive amount of debt we have been burdened with for decades. All along the way, people are trying to prevent us from learning.

This is completely intentional. If we are not provided with the resources to succeed, we will be far less likely to do so.

If we are overburdened by debt and under-educated, we are too focused on survival to reform the system.

Let's start with how we have increased the responsibilities we place on school systems and our expectations for them and our children, all the while with diminishing resources. It has been apparent for decades that people want to reform the educational system in the U.S. because of our perceived poor performance relative to the rest of the world. Unfortunately, our answer to this problem has been to shrink their resources or allow them to stagnate. This is a recipe for disaster.

One of the main talking points of the last couple of decades is that we need to return the U.S. to a time when it was better than it is now. If you are talking about the time when we had free college tuition and universal childcare, I would agree that those policies need to be reinstated because those kinds of policies allowed for education to be accessible. They allowed us the freedom to get an education and put that education to use. They set our country up for huge success.

Let's look at what made the middle class successful for previous generations. It was largely the education they received, in addition to numerous workplace reforms. When the middle class was strong, we focused on educating them on their needed skills, which allowed the middle class to grow and develop. This brought a highly skilled workforce that grew the economy and helped us become the world leader in scientific and technological development.

The U.S. had an enormous industrial base, and many people would like us to return to that way of life. Because, as we will talk about later, people like to feel productive. However, the life of an industrialized nation is far behind us for many reasons, including technological, safety, and economic reasons. We are no longer a predominately industrial-based economy; we are currently an information-based economy. This requires a different type and level of education, and the next economy will require a new set of skills.

As such, new skills need to be developed. If we take the lead in math and science, like we have previously, then we need to invest in public schools. The smarter and better qualified we can make our kids, the easier it will be for them to lift themselves up. If we set our children up for success, then our country will continue to be successful in the future.

As with the argument that guns can protect you from oppression, an education does the same. It may not be as flashy as a gun, but it is far more effective at maintaining a free population. An educated population can see our system's problems and work to fix them. They have the tools to gather the resources they need to survive.

Instead, we have been taking the opposite approach. Instead of providing our teachers with the resources they need, we shift funding to private schools or, at worst, start burning books. Instead of teaching kids about our history, we pass legislation preventing the teaching of anything negative about our past.

Degrading our educational institutions or ensuring that people are overburdened with debt after receiving that education ensures that they can be easily taken advantage of or do not have the resources to fix the system. If they are overburdened with debt, they must accept any position available rather than finding one in their chosen career path or will accept whatever compensation they can get.

Consider how much we have eroded our educational institutions over the last few decades. We have kept teacher pay at poverty levels while requiring master's degrees (which means more debt). We either do a fundraiser or have them pay for the materials they need in their classes, and we generally treat them very poorly. How many other careers must bring all the resources to do their jobs?

If our politicians can keep us from being educated, it will be easier to prevent us from working together. If we are never taught to think critically, how can we see when we are being manipulated. If our media ensures we only learn one side, it's easy to keep us divided. That's part of why so many efforts are to degrade our educational establishments.

How about we put this in perspective. The people that we pay to ensure that our children receive an education and are ready to enter society earn about 20% less than people with similar levels of education, and nearly 20% of them need a second job to survive. In addition, they are frequently not provided with enough supplies for teaching and must have fundraisers to get those supplies.

We demand a lot of our teachers. Recently, in the middle of a pandemic, we asked them to learn all new skills to teach our kids from home and everything else. Then, when we could finally go back to school, the same educators that care for our children were attacked for wanting to implement basic safety measures in their classrooms.

We need to take better care of our teachers, and while it is a nice gesture to donate needed supplies to our local schools, it is more important to pay attention to local budgets and ensure that our schools have the funds they need to receive the pay and resources that they need. Teachers have an enormous impact on the future of our nation, and they get into this career field because of how much they care about children and the future. Providing them with the necessary resources will directly impact how successful our future generations will be.

Currently, the education of our populace, up through high school, is primarily funded through property taxes. This has led to a lot of disparity in the education our children receive, and like I mention throughout the book, this is a feature of our system, not a bug. But that doesn't mean that we must accept it.

Moving past high school onto higher education, whether getting an associate's degree or a doctorate, the requirements of this world are changing to require a higher and more specialized level of education. We need doctors and nurses; we need programmers and people specializing in big data and artificial intelligence. These career fields need people that are highly educated.

So, let's move over to the issue hindering us regarding higher education and student loan debt. Several issues compound to make the student loan debt into the crisis it has become. First, tuition in the U.S. has been rising astronomically since the 1980s.

Over time our assistance to college students has also changed from offering free tuition to Pell grants, where the government would help low- and middle-income students, to student loans. This transition took place along with fewer funds from the government to schools which transferred the payment for education to the students.

This combined to set up the largest sector of debt that this country has, student loan debt, which is larger than mortgages or auto loans. We have been shackling people with loans they can't get rid of that prevent them from engaging in the lives previous generations had access to. Because of this debt, they are prevented from taking out mortgages and other loans simply because they cannot afford them.

Student loan debts are a relatively new thing, which is why older people may not understand why newer generations have to get them. People of previous generations entered the workforce without this debt because tuition used to be free or affordable. People of previous generations would have their college paid for so they could enter the workforce without debt.

We have made an economy that needs higher education to succeed and tell our children they need to go to college. Then we blame them for taking on the loans they need to get this education. Loans that previous generations never needed to get.

Next is that people cannot get rid of this debt by filing for bankruptcy. These loans stay with people, even if they are the reason that people go bankrupt in the first place. The second is that the Department of Education is now responsible for giving out these bank loans to students. Which means they set the terms of the loans. This also means that the Department of Education became the largest lender in the country. For those that want to limit the size and scope of the government, this should be another reason to get rid of student loans and go back to making higher education more affordable.

Educating the citizenry is extremely important, regardless of whether you look at it from the standpoint of national defense, morally good, or just economically. Education makes them harder to fool, teaches them how to look at things analytically, and contributes greatly to the economic wellbeing of our country. Education provides them with the opportunity for success.

One thing we can do is get involved at the state levels to make sure that the disparity between rich and poor school districts is not so great that the poor kids do not have enough equipment or teachers to learn effectively. Is paying slightly higher taxes worth it if you increase the education and wealth of everyone in the state? See what your state universities are doing about tuition and making college affordable. At a federal level, you can pressure your politicians to reform the student loan programs. Having an educated populace will set us up for a huge amount of success in the future. This country has enormous dreams for the future, but we need to educate our citizens to get there.

Before we move on, I want to talk about vocational schools. For those not aware, this is training to perform specific types of careers, such as plumbing, electrical, machine work, and carpentry. These types of jobs always have and will always be very valuable and useful for our society. This type of work will always need to get done; there are not enough people currently performing these tasks. This world is constantly evolving and growing, but these types of careers will always be around.

We have been undermining education in our country for decades. Taking away funding for public schools, piling on debt for those that go to college. This is robbing not only them but our entire country of a successful future. We need to ensure that we provide people with the opportunity to succeed and remove as many barriers as possible.

Chapter Thirteen

Fair compensation for your labor

Most of us believe that holding a job in the U.S. should provide us with enough to live a life. Maybe not one of excess, but enough to afford the basic necessities. Unfortunately, for too many people, that is not a reality. For many more people, while they can afford the basics, a missed paycheck would still throw them into poverty.

Let's start with a basic truth; people like to work. I won't go into the philosophical discussion of what that means since books have been written on that subject, but people like to feel that they are producing something meaningful. Unfortunately, many of us have been fed the lie that people, specifically poor people, are lazy. Generally, those of us that get that message are through media that benefits from polarizing us, preventing us from recognizing the problem, much less doing anything to change it.

Let's start with one of the easy ways that the topic of income is intentionally distorted to keep us from solving this problem. The argument surrounding increasing the minimum wage is supported by a majority of people on both sides, which spawns the distortion of facts. The first is that 1.4 million jobs would be gone if we raised the minimum wage. Here is the thing that is probably true, but here is where semantics are very important. These same polls do not say that unemployment will go up.

How is that? In no state does the current minimum wage allow an adult to pay for the minimum amount to live. This means that in a normal 40-hour workweek, a person earning minimum wage cannot afford to pay their rent, bills, and food. In essence, they cannot live off of this wage. In order to survive, they regularly need to work more than one job.

This is how those two facts are used to distort the discussion. If the minimum wage is raised to the point that people can live off one job, they can quit all the extra jobs they have to survive. That is where job losses come from; people are quitting jobs, and no longer must work just to survive. But remember, this is just the minimum wage. When it was first introduced, it was enough for a worker to support a family and have a decent life. We're not even talking to that standard yet. Let's start talking about paying people what their labor is worth.

An argument quite frequently used against us when we want fair compensation is that our prices may go up on the products we buy, AKA inflation. Of course, this is a fair concern, and we have recently been dealing with a great deal of inflation recently, which has ensured we all received a pay cut.

However, this doesn't bear out. Several causes come to light looking at the reasons for the most recent spike in inflation. Despite what some media outlets may say, none of the reasons is people demanding to be compensated for their labor. Our economies had to shut down for a pandemic slowly.

Then when businesses started to open up again, we could start purchasing goods and services, which created a demand that wasn't there for several years and therefore not enough supply to meet it, raising prices. Additionally, looking at the record-breaking corporate profits that have been coming in during this time, it's easy to see that some companies took advantage of the opportunity to raise prices and make more money. Blaming inflation on the workers is just a way to make us turn on one another.

The argument that it's the worker's fault does not bear out in normal times. Look at Sam's and Costco. Costco pays their workers more than Sam's and even offers them healthcare. Sam's pays less and encourages people to get healthcare from the government. But the prices are practically the same. The same applies when you look at other companies and some of their competition. Suppose a company does not compensate their employees for their labor and encourages them to get government benefits. In that case, that company is indirectly taking tax dollars, again our money, to run their company. Ensuring that companies fairly compensate their employees through wages and benefits would require them to no longer need government services.

Let us look at it another way, just from a purely economic standpoint, if these people have more money and the time to spend it, they can spend it, which means that they can contribute to the local economy. Also, if they are not working all the time, they can be there for their family more frequently and help to raise their children, making them more productive members of society. Too many of us are not being fairly compensated while trying to raise a family.

Check.

This makes the first ask for this chapter to ensure we create a society that ensures people are fairly compensated for their labor, enabling them to survive off one full-time job. Although most people want to work and earn a living, we should not punish them for not having the "right" job.

We would think that this would be easy. Most of us agree that it should be done, and it has been done in other capitalist countries. But unfortunately, many rich people are going to the media to convince us that fairly compensating their workers is a bad idea. I was talking about this at the beginning of the book with people trying to manipulate us into taking actions that would ultimately hurt us. Most of us agree that fairly compensating workers would be a good idea and would help us. But the lie continues that this will be bad. Fairly compensating people for their labor would be a bad idea and make them dependent upon it. This argument has been used against things like the child tax credit, universal healthcare, and tuition-free college, all things we used to have in our country but were taken away.

This argument is so cartoonishly evil that it was used as the villain's motivation in the movie *Mad Max: Fury Road.* In case you have not seen the movie, the bad guy has all the food and water. He gets to dish it out however he would like and prevents the masses from accessing this vital, life-giving resource. His argument for doing so was the same used above that the people should not have access to water because they will become "dependent upon it and grow to resent its absence."

This seems like a cartoonish argument, but too many people are using this as the ultimate theme of their arguments against raising fair compensation for their workers. But this argument does its job of confusing the issue and preventing politicians from both parties from moving forward with the action. Plus, politicians are not motivated to make the change with all the money in politics. Those of us on the left and the right agree that people should receive fair compensation, but politicians from both parties are very reluctant to make the change. This means that this is something that most of us do agree upon, but politicians lack the will to stand up to their donors to get this accomplished. This is another case where they are trying desperately to "wag the dog" by ensuring that we do not actually want to go through with this change.

Union membership is one alternative used in several western countries to ensure that workers receive fair compensation. We will discuss this in more detail later, but basically, the members of a trade join an organization that enables collective bargaining for wages and benefits for their members. Because they advocate so strongly on workers' behalf, there have been many concerted efforts to reduce the strength of unions in the U.S., but many of the advantages we have today, like weekends and 40-hour work weeks, are thanks to them. Strengthening employee groups and enabling them to collectively bargain would also ensure that workers received fair wages and benefits for their labor. That's why the last ask for this chapter is to work with each other to pressure our businesses for fair compensation while we continue to pressure our politicians to stop undermining these efforts.

Chapter Fourteen

Taxes and How Much We Get for What We Pay

The U.S. has a crazy paradox around the amount we are taxed and how the overall amount is deducted from our paychecks. As a percentage of the money that we pay in both taxes and for our benefits, we have a smaller percentage of take-home pay than a lot of other countries. However, these deductions are broken up a lot to obfuscate this fact, there are federal, state, and local income taxes, property taxes, sales taxes, as well as things like social security and Medicare, and then we have to pay for things like healthcare, which does not include vision and dental, those benefits are paid for separately.

So, before we even see our paychecks, a lot has been taken out. This is why so many people do not feel like they are getting a good return for what they are paying. Whenever there is a discussion about raising taxes to pay for things, there is such a huge pushback from many people, particularly middle to low-income individuals.

On the flip side, many companies not only pay no taxes but receive money from the government. To be clear, I do not mean small businesses; I mean companies like Amazon, FedEx, Nike, and Dish.

Let me repeat that, at least 55 large companies did not pay any federal taxes for 2020 but actually got money from the government for an effective tax rate over negative 8.6 per cent. So, that means we gave them money for the services they provided, and then we gave them our tax dollars. So, when we talk about tax rates later on, please keep that in mind. Because while, on paper, the tax rate for these corporations may be higher, what they are actually paying is a far cry from that figure.

This is not the only paradox when it comes to economic equality in the U.S. There are, as of this writing, over 12 million people in the U.S. that are millionaires. But unfortunately, we also have a tremendous number of people, 44 million, below the poverty line.

In researching this book, I have learned many things; one of the more frustrating is that there are at least 1 trillion dollars in taxes that we cannot collect because of tax avoidance schemes written into our tax code. To put this in perspective, the annual U.S. budget has a shortfall of 0.9 trillion. That means if people paid what they owed, there would be a surplus. That means that even if we kept the same percentages for taxed income, we would have a surplus. But we do not because there are too many loopholes. I will bring this back up when we get to the ask of the section.

Since government budgets usually get compared to household budgets in discussions that take place in the media, let's talk about budgets. Firstly, your spending is a reflection of your priorities balanced against your regular income. Your household budget probably reflects the importance of providing food and shelter for your family. Then, where you can, you do other things with it. For example, some of us buy games, go on trips, or even further our education. Some of us spend money going towards charities. Thank you for spending some of your money on this book.

Similarly, as a country, our budget also reflects our priorities. We should care deeply about how our tax dollars are spent because that is our money. I know a lot of us are aware of this, but sometimes it helps to break things down to the simplest state. Looking at our government budgets, we can see what we prioritize at a local, state, and federal level.

Now, let's talk about deficit spending, i.e., spending more money than is in the budget. Because every time there is a discussion about government budgets, especially the federal one, the deficit comes up, and people talk about the size of the debt. To be fair, this is a good thing to be concerned about, but not as big of a problem as we, myself included, have been led to believe.

Let's go back to the example of a household budget before we move to something like a federal budget. Many people agree that our household budget should not have more expenses than it does income, which makes sense on the surface. But really, it is that you should not take on more debt than you can make payments towards. Let me explain.

Have you bought a car? Did you pay for all of it at once, or did you make payments? If you did not pay for it all at once, why did you buy one at all? It was probably because a car would allow you to go to your place of employment or the grocery store for food and supplies.

How about a house? It is probably the same thing. You did not pay for it all at once, but it provided a place for you to make a home. Ideally, home ownership even allows us to create generational wealth for our families.

Let us do something more frivolous. Have you ever taken a vacation? Did you put any of it on credit? If you could not afford to pay for the entirety of the vacation, why did you take it at all? Maybe you saved up ahead of time or paid it off over time.

All these examples are of times that you may personally have gone into debt or did not have the money to pay for a thing in its entirety upfront. But you still made that purchase because the debt was manageable.

Government budgets are like that. They may not have the money at the moment to build the roads that the community needs, but the infrastructure will allow people to get to their place of employment and, in turn, generate more income for the government. Debt, in and of itself, is not a scary thing. However, mismanaging it or not being able to pay for it is worrying. Besides, if a government had all of the money it ever needed to pay for the projects it took on as a whole, I am sure many of us would want our tax money back.

This section is one of those that, despite what our media tells us, most of us agree upon. We primarily support a progressive tax system (i.e., people with more money pay more taxes), that we need to prioritize our government budgets that take care of our priorities without taking on too large of a debt burden, and that we need to simplify our tax system. Additionally, when we look at the totality of taxes that we pay, we agree that we pay a lot but do not always get a good return on investment.

Part of this conversation needs to focus on the intentional distortions that prevent us from understanding these conversations and finding common ground. For example, we hear how conservatives think that liberals want to tax billionaires into oblivion. But this is one of many things that are said to divide us and not listen to one another.

Let's explain a progressive tax policy by describing how federal income taxes work in the United States. First, note that this is an oversimplification and is only about federal income taxes, not state or locality taxes, property, sales taxes, or any other deduction from our paychecks. Also, the numbers used are just used for this example and are not the real ones, just for the ease of understanding them and to keep the math simple.

A progressive tax means that the more you earn, the more you pay, but it is not always as clear-cut to understand. If someone who earns over $250,000 pays 35% in taxes, that is true for a percentage of their income. Basically, the first $10,000 is taxed at 10%, then the money from $10,001 until $40,000 is taxed at 12%, then from $40,001 until $80,000 the tax rate is 22%. Again, these are rounded to simplify the math. So for someone making $75,000 a year, $10,000 is taxed at 10%, for $1,000, $30,000 is taxed at 12%, for $3,600, and $35,000 is taxed at 22%, for $7,700. This is a total of $12,300, which is an effective tax rate of 16.4%.

That is not too bad, but there is an issue beyond the overall complexity of the federal, in that many of the wealthiest do not pay taxes. One point that comes up about this is that most income from income taxes is from the wealthiest people, which is true. After all, they earn the most money, so they pay the most.

When we look at just the federal income tax, it looks pretty manageable despite the problems, but that is not the entire picture. All sorts of taxes get tacked on, like state income taxes, sales taxes, or property taxes. All of which can lead to a very confusing mess.

For now, let's look at some of the intentional misrepresentations around Social Security. There have been many media outlets and politicians on the right saying that it has been going bankrupt for decades and have been recently calling it an entitlement. First, it is not an entitlement. We all pay into that for our entire working career. Social Security was never meant as an entitlement. It is literally our money, and not in an abstract way that all tax money is the people's money. We paid for that. That is like saying your retirement fund is an entitlement. It is not; you paid for that too.

One thing that we have been told for decades now is, "Social Security is going bankrupt?" Well, that is true now, but it wasn't before. Why is it true now?

Here is a shock, but a few decades ago, a very famous politician lied to convince the public that it was going bankrupt and that the government should be able to access the funds. Then, politicians from both parties saw this huge amount of money coming in and decided to spend it. So now it has financial problems, but only because politicians lied to us to steal it.

To repeat the point, this is not limited to just one political party; it is both of them. Yes, one of them started the problem, but neither one of them fixed it. They were not supposed to be able to touch the money since, again, it is ours, but they did. So now they're trying to tell us there isn't enough since they've taken it.

This is something that I think all of us would love to fix. The alternative is that it goes broke, and while I know that some of us have been convinced that is a good thing, think about how many of our family members depend upon social security, either because they retired or because of medical issues.

If we want to fix this, we need to have our politicians work to get it done. All of us. Because the moment one of us stands up to say that this needs to be fixed, the other party is going to say that it does not need to be public.

Now let us move on to sales taxes. This is simple and is just the tax that is on the things that we buy. However, as we would expect, this tax mainly affects the people who buy the most, which affects poorer people the most as a percentage of income. That's why people call this a regressive tax, especially when politicians start talking about raising them.

Lastly, let's talk about property taxes. Many local governments use them to pay for things like school systems. Now, while I talk about some of the disparities, this causes in another section of the book, here I want to discuss something else.

Specifically, when you buy a house, who owns that property? For the purpose of this discussion, I'm not talking about the bank.

If you completely pay off the mortgage to your house, you still owe property taxes. Here is the question, though, what happens if we don't, or can't, pay those taxes? What if we receive a house from a relative, or the tax rate goes above what we can pay? What should happen to that house? Currently, many systems are designed to lose your house if you don't pay that tax. So while the things it pays for may be an important way to invest in our communities, should the government be able to take our homes because of a tax?

Okay, I think we have had enough of a primer about taxes in the United States. I did not cover them all, and certainly not all of the deductions we have, and I think that would be a waste of time to continue because that is not the point of this chapter. The point is to look at things we agree upon. The first of which is that most people feel like their taxes are not being spent in the right way. The second is that most of us are paying a lot of overall taxes, while those at the top aren't paying nearly enough. The third is that our tax code is needlessly complicated. Plus, to add to the excitement of the last point, it is very complicated, yet if we get it wrong, we go to prison.

While there are some points that we agree upon, there are some very important differences. First, how about we look at the major agreement that our tax structure is way too complicated. Most people would love for our income taxes to be easy enough to complete on a postcard. Some even advocate for the IRS to submit our tax statement for us to review instead of the other way around. This works since they already have our data and would prevent people from going to jail for making a mistake. Additionally, it would prevent tax evasion, costing the U.S. hundreds of billions of dollars annually.

Taxes should be simple, and since the government already has our data, we should not go to jail for not correctly navigating an overly complex tax code. Plus, we both think that we should get what we pay for. Taxes are an investment. They are an investment we make in the future success of our country.

We like things like roads, the police, and fire departments. However, taxes pay for a lot of the infrastructure we all use to move ourselves and our goods and services. They pay for the parks we all use and congregate for fun. Taxes pay for the public schools that we use, which keeps us an educated populace.

We also pay taxes for some healthcare services, like Medicare and Medicaid. Again, note that I did not include Social Security here because that is something you pay for that you earn. The government says they do not have enough to fund it because they stole it from you.

Our governments need to have an income to provide for the services we expect them to provide. Here is another point where I think we might be able to agree. Do you think it is right that companies like Google and Amazon pay zero in federal taxes? By the way, this is not an argument to overtax these companies; they just need to pay taxes, especially since they benefit from the systems our taxes have paid for.

There has been an explosion of support for politicians and wealthy people who have not paid taxes. How does that make any sense whatsoever? I know people claim that these people avoiding taxes are brilliant, but they are really exploiting the system and convincing people their scam is beneficial when it is, in fact, hurting the communities in which they live.

The companies that do not pay their taxes are reaping the benefits of past investments we have made as a country while making none of their own. The investments made by previous generations are what enabled those infrastructure projects to be built. If these companies are not paying taxes, they are not investing in the future success of our country or themselves.

How about we use Amazon as an example. They use the roads that were built using taxes, they use the postal service, a public service, they use the educated workers that our school system creates, and their business model is based on the internet, whose invention was enabled because of tax dollars.

They are having enormous success using the resources our taxes have built for them, and they have not been helping to support the same system. Now here is the thing. It is not Amazon's fault that they didn't invest in the system that made them successful. They are playing by the rules of the system. The system is designed this way and has been for a while. We must fix the system so that others can have the opportunity to succeed.

Another example of exploiting the system is the hedge fund billionaires that have made their money while paying a minimal number of taxes. For those unaware, these people make their money from trading on the stock market. They do not produce anything, they do not create anything, and beyond a small number of assistants, they do not create jobs.

Now, while I do not begrudge them for using the system we built to make money, they are doing so without investing in the system that helped them build their wealth. Also, some people have argued that raising their contribution will discourage them from investing. Warren Buffet had the best response to that argument, saying that if taxes prevent you from investing, you're in the wrong business. Of course, this is paraphrasing a much longer statement, but the takeaway is that if someone is not investing, then they are not making money, regardless of taxes.

Let's talk about that system for a minute; when people look back to when this country was doing well and had a strong middle class, our tax system invested in our country. It invested in education and infrastructure. The taxes were so high on companies that it made practical business sense to invest in their employee's pay, expand their businesses, or research and development. But unfortunately, we decided a few decades ago to try a different path where instead of incentivizing people and companies to reinvest in themselves and their companies, we incentivized them to fire their employees and overcompensate executives.

We decided that we would stop investing in education and infrastructure. We decided to stop investing in protecting our middle class. This decision was 'trickle-down economics.' This is when we stopped investing in our people and hoped that rich people would 'trickle-down wealth to the rest of the population. But there was no incentive for them to reinvest in the system that made them successful, so instead, they hoarded their wealth.

This idea that these mega-wealthy corporations took advantage of is the flawed economic theory of 'trickle-down economics.' For those who do not know, this theory believes that if you give the richest people money, it will trickle down to the rest of the population. It is flawed for several very obvious reasons, as well as a few less obvious ones.

The biggest flaw is assuming that wealthy people have limited ways to hold onto money. Therefore, if we give them more money, it will be enough at some point, and they will treat their employees better. I am not sure how anyone believed that, but let's use Jeff Bezos as an example, he has been vying for the title of richest man alive for a while now, but as his wealth has gone up, the wealth of his employees has not.

Again, he is succeeding in the system the way it is designed. There is minimal public pressure to take better care of his employees, but no requirement to pay them or even allow them bathroom breaks. His treatment of employees shows how the system is not working for most people.

One of the less obvious flaws in this theory is in looking at how people spend money. Rich, middle-class, and poor people spend money differently. Poor people spend money on necessities. They need food, shelter, and safety. Middle-class people tend to have their basic needs met, so they spend their money having experiences. This is also where most small business owners are in this spectrum. Rich people do all this and have money left to save a lot.

While I know this is a simplification, the overlying point is that the poor and middle class spend a larger percentage of their incomes directly on the local economies. The rich save a lot of their money or put it into something that does not continually stimulate the economy. The circulation of money in our economies keeps it running.

We will also touch on this point in a few other places throughout the book, but it bears repeating here. By setting up the system this way, companies are not inclined to take care of their employees. How many large companies pay poverty wages? How many large companies do not provide their employees with healthcare but expect their employees to get healthcare from the government? How many billionaires are making money off the investment we made into the system (via taxes) without paying into it themselves? Is that just?

Think about it this way: the time people like to think of when the U.S. was great, we were able to invest in infrastructure and education and go to the moon, and the marginal tax rate on the wealthiest was in the 80-90%. Now, I know that sounds like a lot, and it is, but it is not; I repeat, NOT 80-90% of their total wealth or income. As discussed above, this is only the amount taxed on income earned above a certain level. They were still very wealthy.

This all changed when we decided to embrace the policy of "trickle-down" economics starting in the late 1980s. These policies have done a phenomenal job of transferring Trillions of dollars' worth of wealth to the top 1% of the country because money stopped flowing into our economy. There was no incentive to put that money into research and development or the expansion of factories. Our current tax structure enforces this and encourages hoarding wealth by encouraging stock buybacks. This further prevents money from flowing into the economy at large.

There is a correlation between removing wealth from the populace and our inability to do massive infrastructure projects since creating these changes. The same applies to our inability to raise teachers' wages in a meaningful way.

Most of us do not mind rich people being rich. But I understand the anger many people have towards them, especially when they do not invest in the system that made them successful by not paying taxes.

What is the ask for this section? We should ensure that our wealthiest citizens are paying their fair share and fairly compensating their employees. This includes closing loopholes that prevent them from paying the taxes they owe or even giving them money from the taxpayers. While I am not going to get into what tax policies I think are the absolute best, the policies we currently have in place are not sufficient. They enable the wealthiest to not invest in the system that allowed them to generate their wealth.

Our tax codes are a labyrinth nearly impossible for regular people to navigate and punish us for the slightest error. However, since our taxes are our investment in our government, we should be able to understand them and where they are going.

We should be able to keep most of the money we work for, taxes should be simple and equitable, and we should receive a good return on our investment. Right now, our tax code is none of those things, and neither party wants to clean it up. Instead, they would rather have us fight one another.

Chapter Fifteen

Healthcare Ensures Personal Freedom

Based on the discourse we hear a lot of our political and media figures use to talk about healthcare in the U.S., it seems odd to have this in a section about commonalities. Most of the people on the right and left agree on what needs to be done to fix our healthcare system. But the way these arguments are framed in our media distorts these discussions so that we don't support one another. We need to take action that provides healthcare to our citizens, even if we argue about the way to get there. Many of us understand that without healthcare, we don't have the freedom and autonomy necessary to do anything else with our lives.

There are a lot of great points made by both sides of the political spectrum about our healthcare system that does not get heard because it is easier to demonize those that do not agree with us. As I will point out throughout this book, preventing us from hearing one another is currently a feature, not a bug, of our system. So, I will acknowledge the points that both sides make in this matter while trying to get us to see the other side as well. In the end, I hope that we can work together to develop the best model that gets us the healthcare we all desperately need.

The main problem is that many people do not have healthcare, or they must worry about going broke for any medical expenses, or they are forced to choose another necessity, such as food, over their medicine. This leaves many people without healthcare or forces them to remain in poverty. Neither of the options would we want for ourselves or those close to us.

We all recognize that the cost of healthcare is out of control in the U.S., and many want us to have something akin to European healthcare. However, those of us who have had healthcare provided by the U.S. Government or had access to European healthcare know that there are valid concerns, usually raised by those on the right, that need to be addressed with this care system. Moving forward, these concerns would need to be addressed rather than used to prevent us from fixing a broken system. Otherwise, we either keep what we have, which is broken, or we move to a new system that is broken in new and interesting ways.

There are two major hurdles to address in terms of ensuring that we have the healthcare needed: cost and quality. We know that the cost can be pretty low for those of us who have served in the military. Even hyper-partisan studies on the right, like those done by the Koch brothers, have shown that government-run healthcare would save billions of dollars and that each of us would save thousands of dollars a year paying for the tax instead of paying for all the various types of insurance.

Those that hyper-partisan groups conducted on the left showed even more savings and cost reductions. Either way, the point is clear that our current system is costing each of us an incredible amount of money. Money that could be spent gives us the freedom to do activities we enjoy. Currently, we pay an incredible amount of money for our healthcare, and most people don't want that to stay the same, or worse, increase.

This brings us to the question of the quality of medical care. In the U.S., we currently enjoy a very high level of quality medical care and innovation. It is this specific hurdle that I would like us to understand so that we can work together to come up with a better system.

I would like for those on the right and the left to come up with a reasonable way of ensuring that we have quality, innovative healthcare while keeping costs low. Help each other see that we need to incorporate ways to continue innovating and that it's this innovation that makes us a world leader. However, we cannot rely upon this level of innovation as the sole reason to keep our current state of healthcare.

Another problem with our healthcare system is that those who can afford insurance subsidize those who can't afford it. This is in effect at a micro level, when one person can't afford their treatment, to the macro when our healthcare costs go up to subsidize lower costs in other countries. This is further exacerbated when some of the wealthiest companies do not provide their U.S. employees with insurance forcing them to use government insurance anyway, like Walmart and McDonald's. Note that their employees in other countries do have insurance.

For those of us that did not know that some of the largest companies are already not providing healthcare, that can come as a surprise, but some of the wealthiest companies in the world are not providing healthcare to their employees and are encouraging them to use government-provided resources. There is a solution to solve this problem for these larger companies, which also solves the insurance problem for much smaller businesses as well, providing a single-payer option through the government.

Providing a single-payer option solves the problem of companies not offering insurance to their employees. Plus, this doesn't just apply to large companies; it can also apply to small ones. Many of us support small businesses and their need for full-time employees. Relieving them of the major expense of providing healthcare for their employees will greatly help those smaller businesses succeed. They can hire full-time workers without having to take on that additional expense. Untying healthcare from employment can help our small businesses thrive. Which, in turn, will help the communities in which they live.

An additional problem having a public option would solve the lack of healthcare options that are within the current 'gig economy.' For those of us unfamiliar with this, the 'gig economy' has people working numerous jobs, with none of them being required to offer healthcare, will be able to get the care that they need. Providing freedom and flexibility to both the company and the employees.

Additionally, one of the reasons our healthcare is so expensive is that we subsidize many of the other countries that have universal care. This is because they can collectively bargain on drug prices, while the U.S. does not and, in some cases, is not allowed to do so. This means that we will always have more expensive care as long as we are unable to bargain.

What I am asking for all of us is that we become a part of the conversation that helps our family members that are already receiving government-run healthcare get better care while we get to keep a lot more of our money. This will help us all enjoy more of the freedom we deserve.

Before we leave this section, how about we cover a couple of additional lies about this topic, the first is that allowing everyone accesses to healthcare will make doctors poorer or damage the industry as a whole.

What do you think about lawyers? Are they doing well off? Is the legal profession being diminished? Why am I talking about lawyers? Well, our constitution, the 6th amendment, ensures that everyone can access legal defense. Now, granted, there are problems with public defenders being overworked, but including their necessity in the constitution did not bankrupt the entire industry. Likewise, ensuring healthcare for everyone won't automatically destroy the industry.

The other lie concerns the Affordable Care Act (ACA). The lie about this is that it is an idea from the left. It was passed on the federal level by the Democratic Party, but it was a copy of a conservative state policy implemented by a Republican governor. Now, there are lots of problems with the ACA, but it is in no way a liberal or left-leaning concept.

Our healthcare system needs to be fixed; I think most of us agree upon that. We need to have better collective bargaining to lower our drug prices so an individual company does not have to argue with the European Union about the cost of a drug. We need to ensure that everyone has a basic level of healthcare so that both hospitals do not have to increase their prices for people that can pay to cover caring for people that cannot. We also need to keep a high level of innovation. None of these things is mutually exclusive. We can do all of it. Lots of us agree upon that, so the ask is that we need to convince the legislators to do something. Whether at the state or federal level, this is a problem that needs to be addressed sooner rather than later. Otherwise, we will continue to waste our money on a broken system, people will continue to go destitute trying to pay for these bills, and others will still die from the lack of access to the care they need.

Chapter Sixteen

Employment Rights

We just finished discussing the need to ensure that we have the income and healthcare to ensure that we have the freedom to live our lives, but what about other aspects of our employees that would help us maximize our freedoms. We talked about how the employment demands of the future are going to be vastly different from the needs of the past and how we need to address them with education. We spoke about how strengthening unions would be an effective alternative to the minimum wage. But many other freedoms we do not have, which many other countries enjoy routinely. There is no reason we can't have those same freedoms.

We all like weekends, even if they are too short. They give us time to spend with our families, to work on projects around the house, or the time to relax and just enjoy the downtime. However, we also do not mind working a 40-hour work week. We like to feel that we have a sense of accomplishment in our lives. So why am I talking about these things in the section on employment rights? Well, these are a couple of things that were brought to us from the power of unions, aka, when we worked together.

Now, unions get a bad reputation, some of which deservedly so, which we will touch on later, but they have had a net positive outcome on our society and our work/life balance. But unfortunately, despite the positive effects that unions have had upon our lives, they have fallen out of power within the last few decades.

So much power has been removed from employees that companies are allowed to fire employees for even discussing starting a union in many states, or they are incentivized to close plants and factories if their employees start a union. One of the lies that makes this possible is that we've all been told that being anti-union somehow means you are pro-business. This is apparent in how laws such as "Right to Work" remove our power as employees.

Some people in politics and the media have argued against employers providing healthcare and raising the minimum wage by stating that each person needs to stand up for themselves and leave a job that doesn't take care of them. They then go on to argue against the concept of a union because the person should not have to depend upon a union for assistance. This merely sets the person up to take the blame for the jobs and benefits available in their community. People must still function in our society and can only make choices with available options. If there are no jobs with good pay or benefits in their area, how are they supposed to change that by themselves?

To be fair, it makes sense that a company would provide the minimum pay and benefits that an employee will accept. If all the company wants to do is make money, what incentive is there to pay employees more or ensure their health and welfare. Additionally, if these companies can get the politicians on their side, then they can call our state a 'Right to Work' state, which means the exact opposite. For those that do not know, a 'Right to Work' state means that they can fire their employees without cause. It does not mean we have any protections, which the title implies.

These efforts are trying to take us back to a model we have tried in the U.S. of uncontrolled capitalism, where the company owns everything about an employee, where they live, work, shop, and go to school. Then, they were called company towns and controlled the entire environment their workers lived in, including the shops, schools, and churches. Now they are called things like "Innovation Zones." So, while I am going to say some negative things about unions, the idea of uncontrolled capitalism removes our rights to move, speak, think, and believe freely in our homes and communities.

Ok, so I have talked positively about unions for a bit, so how about we talk about some of the negative sides as well. They are prone to corruption within the organization and how they handle visible external problems. Recently the United Auto Workers just settled a corruption case being brought against them. Additionally, other unions have had a bad habit of protecting members that underperform or, in some cases, conduct outright illegal activities. In the case of the Saturn automotive company, unions were one of the leading factors that drove it out of business. This means that unions have successfully sunk companies people have relied upon for employment. The same corruption that can infect our political systems can infect union leadership if left unchecked.

Here is the problem, employees need protection, as we initially talked about. There are too many employees that are currently being abused and exploited solely so the company can make more money. Again, I will use Amazon as an example. The workers in their distribution and packaging centers helped millions of Americans through the pandemic by ensuring they had all the supplies they needed. For this, they were not given bathroom breaks, and they received a minimal amount of pay. I pick on Amazon because there are numerous examples of employees being mistreated, but they are not the only ones conducting such activities.

Another way that employees need protection is from wage theft. If you are not aware of what that is, it is when an employer does not pay you what you are owed. In other words, people don't get paid for their labor. Plus, this disproportionately affects those least able to combat this theft. In 2019 alone, over $9 billion was taken from employees making less than $13 an hour. Plus, because of legal employment policies, the employer can't sue or take their company to court for the stolen wages. Therefore, they have no one who can look out for them to prevent this behavior or get their wages back.

Employees need someone to look out for them and ensure they are taken care of and not mistreated. There are few legal recourses for them to stand up for their rights singularly. Alternatively, the company needs to make sure that they stay in business. So, how do we take care of the employees while ensuring that the business remains healthy and strong?

Ideally, this is where a union comes into play. They provide a means for employees to collectively work together and bargain for things like higher pay, healthcare, retirements, training, and safety. They can also ensure that people are not fired without cause or because they are close to retirement (if a company gets rid of you before you can retire, they do not have to pay retirement benefits; unfortunately, this still happens).

But what happens when a union prevents a company from growing or prevents a dangerous employee from being fired? What happens when the union itself is corrupt? In much of this, there are policies in place within the company on how to deal with the union and the problems that it faces. However, sometimes an outside agency needs to get involved, and the FBI gets involved in cases of corruption. We can also take a proactive role in voting for new leadership to ensure they do not get corrupted like our political leadership.

We need a way to ensure that employees are protected while maintaining a business's ability to grow. This is not a new problem and has been solved in a lot of other countries, usually through a mixture of unions and regulations. However, the landscape of work has perpetually changed. It looks very different now than when many of us originally entered the workforce. Each change comes with its own strengths and weaknesses. Regardless, we need to ensure that the employees who run our businesses are protected.

So here is my ask for this section, find out about the laws protecting employees in your states because many of them are different. Find out if there are unions in your field, and if there are, look into what it would take to be a member. While there can be some problems with unions, the benefits they provide to their members and the rest of society far outweigh those problems. In addition to the earlier examples, they also ensured that we no longer allow child labor. In the future, unions could ensure that we have benefits like maternity and paternity leave. No employee can stand up to an employer refusing to pay them or treat them with respect, but all of us standing up together can make that possible.

Chapter Seventeen

All Citizens Should be Allowed to Vote

While other sections have had to deal with a lot of misconceptions or misunderstandings, this one is different. A lot of lies have been told in this arena that need to be corrected. Lies are told to undermine our system. Lies are told to make us lose faith in our institutions.

Let me say this right out of the gate. Voting fraud in the United States is exceedingly rare. As a percentage, it is next to zero. Plus, the claim that the 2020 election is false or that there was massive voter fraud is a lie.

Unfortunately, while voter fraud is exceedingly rare, voter suppression is incredibly and increasingly common. However, if we are told that voter fraud is a huge problem, then the efforts to suppress votes make sense as a solution. If we are told that voting can't be trusted, we lose faith in those institutions and are less likely to vote. This is one of the ways that politicians are ensuring that we no longer have the power to police them. As a result, many of them do not want to work for us, and they use tools like voter suppression and gerrymandering to ensure that they do not.

The recounts by groups with no experience in elections or election fraud, such as the one in Arizona, are an effort to make us lose faith in our voting system. They continued to ensure that people lost faith in the voting system for so long. Not everyone, but enough people, so that when the next election is called into doubt, more people will lose faith in voting and, therefore, the government.

When thinking about voting, two questions should be at the forefront. First, do politicians work for us, or do we work for them? Many politicians would have us believe it is the latter. This is the problem of gerrymandering that we will be addressing. The second is, should everyone be legally allowed to vote to have the opportunity to vote? I suspect very few of us would say that we should limit the opportunity of those with the right to vote from voting, which is why voter suppression laws are framed in such a way to make it seem like they are just protecting a system.

Removing the opportunity of those legally allowed to vote is the goal of voter suppression laws being worked on throughout this country. First, they tell us that there has been a problem with the election and that there is voter fraud. Then they now have to limit the access to voting by limiting the number of times and places and the people who can vote by only allowing specific types of IDs and placing limits that invalidate the IDs of people they don't want to vote.

So why include this in the section that says we can work together? Our politicians clearly think there is no way for that to happen, but I think there is a way for us to come together. But one thing that joins many of us is that we don't like being told what to do or limiting our rights. There is a fair share of politicians that are attempting to "wag the dog" to keep us from holding them accountable. But, there is a lot of common ground that we share when it comes to making sure that we have fair elections; it is just that some of us view that definition differently.

Let us hit the areas that everyone agrees upon. Gerrymandering is bad, and only citizens should vote. I know that the last one is a shock to some, but that is because our politicians and media have been lying to us and saying that non-citizens have been voting or that one side only wins because of the illegal votes. Those are lies.

Just a quick primer on gerrymandering is when politicians redraw the lines on a map to create districts that ensure they strengthen their chances at political victory and diminish their opponents. Both parties do this by forcing everyone from one party into one district or diluting their opponents by dividing them into lots of districts.

As you can imagine, this practice basically means that politicians are now selecting their voters. This is the exact opposite of a democracy. Unfortunately, this practice is also legal; as long as they phrase their reasoning correctly, politicians can get away with this practice. For example, Republicans in North Carolina openly argued in court that they had gerrymandered their districts to prevent Democrats from having power, despite the Democrats having an equal number of voters. That is one example, but Democrats have done the same tactic too. This is vital because after the census is conducted (every ten years, it was just conducted in 2020), the district lines get redrawn. So, this issue is one that is constantly coming up or is currently taking place. Regardless of when this occurs, we must ensure that this practice ends. What impetus do politicians have to work for us if they never have to worry about our vote?

So, what is the next step they need to take to ensure they remain in power? Easy, make sure that the people that do not support their party are unable to vote. That makes sure that the politicians not only pick the places with people that support them, but they also remove the voice of those that do not.

Before we go too far down the rabbit hole of voter suppression, let's talk about voter ID laws and who can vote. First, only citizens can vote, meaning if someone is here illegally, they cannot vote. That already is a thing and always has been a reality. Second, while some states have laxer laws than others, every state ensures that the person voting is legally allowed to vote in that district. Besides, voter ID laws only prevent a form of voter fraud known as 'impersonation fraud,' which, according to the Washington Post, from 2000 until 2014, there have only been "31 credible instances" out of more than one billion votes. Now, I know what I just said will surprise some, especially with certain media outlets talking about dead people and illegal immigrants voting all the time. But these media outlets are being incentivized to make us afraid, as we discussed earlier.

Speaking about some of these lies that are told to manipulate us, one of them is that allowing more votes will only support one party. This lie is so pervasive that Republican lawyers have argued in front of the Supreme Court that the reason they are trying to enact voter suppression laws is that if they do not, they will never be elected again. While it is laughably sad that a particular argument is being used to defend something so reprehensible, it has never been shown that allowing more people to vote only supports one party. Allowing more people to vote holds elected officials accountable, but it does not support one party over the other.

Now, while I was making fun of Republican lawmakers above, Democratic lawmakers are not much better. However, there is an issue that some have had a hard time grasping, election security and the need for paper ballots. Now there is an issue with election security that people often get confused about, paper vs. electronic ballots. Many very capable countries are interested in influencing our elections, either through our media or hacking our systems. So how can we be certain that our votes have been counted fairly? Paper ballots. Now, these can be read by a machine, but this allows for recounts and audits. This makes sure that votes are, in fact, being counted fairly.

There has been legislation brought forward to ensure election integrity and ensure that people have the right, and access, to vote, but politicians are not feeling much pressure actually to get this legislation passed. Suppose we want to improve voting in the country. In that case, we need to pressure our legislators to enact legislation that ensures citizens can vote and that there is accountability within the system. Furthermore, we need to pressure them not to pass or repeal the swath of voter suppression legislation currently in many states. Learn about the laws in your state and the effect they have on voters, then repeal the laws where they do encourage voter suppression.

If we are afraid that more people voting will ensure our politicians will never get elected again, then we either get better ideas or learn how to convey them in a way that people understand. Both sides have good ideas, and both sides also have some crazy people. Stop letting politicians "wag the dog." It is our country; they work for us. If they do not do the job they were hired to do, we fire them in the next election, regardless of party.

Going back to the discussion we had about guns and the right to bear arms, how would we feel if all of the hurdles being put in place for voting were applied to purchasing a gun? If you could only do it a certain way, at a certain time, at a certain place, and had to have multiple forms of ID to prove you were who you said you were, and if there was a mix-up or typo anywhere in the entire process you would be denied? Now, these two debates are different. There are different problems at the heart of each issue. But voting is fundamental to our

Democratic Republic. We must remind our officials that they work for us.

Please note that I did not talk about the Electoral College or all the other ways we could improve the way we could elect officials to represent us better. Instead, I just wanted to focus on the immediate concerns and ways we seem to be backsliding. These concerns would need to be addressed regardless of the system that we use. We should not allow a system that does not give the people a voice in their government.

Many other voter choice systems would help us hold our politicians accountable and get us the representation we desire. We currently use a first-past-the-post method of electing officials, which means that many of us end up holding our noses and voting for someone that is "close enough" to our beliefs or causes the least amount of damage to our system. But there are other methods of voting, such as ranked choice, that allow us to rank who we want in an election, which would allow us more options for choosing our politicians. Other methods would also improve our voting system, but for now, I want to focus on not losing ground.

What can we do? Support each other in removing gerrymandered districts. Democratic and Republican parties have done this and have silenced the voices of people who disagree with them. Second, ensure that our legislators do not suppress votes. Both of these methods are being used to ensure that we do not get a voice. They are used to ensure that we do not hold our elected officials accountable. Do not accept that. So, work together to ensure everyone's voice is heard and that our elected officials work for us, not the other way around.

The ask here is simple: make sure that citizens have an easy time voting, whether that means expanding it over a few days, making it a holiday, expanding mail-in voting, or whatever. The important thing is that the people get heard. Our politicians do not want to hear from us; they want to pick which of our votes and which do not. That is not how either a Democracy or a Republic works. Hold them accountable.

The last thing to ask in this section is for you to vote. We may not have a politician we like on the ballot, but tremendous sacrifices have been made to ensure you can vote. Additionally, if we are ever to hold our politicians accountable, we must vote and show up.

Chapter Eighteen

Guns and the need for self-defense

I will start this with the bottom line up front; this is a tailor-made topic to divide us. We all feel passionate about this subject, no matter what side of the gun debate we adhere to. This is a great subject to use to ensure that we stay divided and keep thinking that the other side is utterly crazy in their line of thought. Therefore, to ensure we can come together and see each other's points, I have some things for all of us to think about on both sides of the argument.

With that in mind, the first point is that no one is coming for your guns. Yes, I am quite aware that the NRA and the media have been telling us this lie for decades in a sometimes-successful effort to convince us that liberals, Democrats, or Leftists, are coming to collect all the guns, but this is a lie. They are not. I am also aware that a subset of the population does not see why we need to own guns, but hopefully, I will be able to explain to them why some of us feel it is very important to own them.

Also, I know that attempts are being made to license gun owners, but that is not the same as trying to take them. When the government gives you a driver's license, it is not a Machiavellian scheme to take your car. So let me repeat this before I go further, there is no vast conspiracy to come and take our guns. The conversation that our media and politicians don't want us to have is how we can reduce the number of people that die from gun violence, including suicides and mass shootings.

This part of the conversation gets ignored because it's scarier and more manipulative to say that people are coming for your guns. Plus, because this fear successfully encourages us to buy more guns, our media and political leaders continue to tell us that "all liberals are coming for our guns" for decades. But many of us have been to a gun range with people we disagree with. So how should we deal with this manipulation? I want all of us to participate in the conversation around guns beyond making fun of people for their gun ownership status or simply saying "no" to anyone that disagrees.

Because if we allow the national conversation around gun ownership to remain as toxic as it is, then the freedom of individual ownership may not hold forever. This unhealthy conversation makes many people turn away from gun ownership. Most people regularly see the effects of gun violence and want to curb it. If we want to engage in a conversation on the topic, we need to listen more to what people are saying rather than a caricature of them portrayed in the media.

So, let's start with some history. The individual right to bear arms has been one of our traditions since the forgone year of 2008. The Supreme Court case of DC vs. Heller was a major change in how the second amendment was interpreted and a huge win for everyone, including those on the left and right ends of the political spectrum.

Prior to this decision, there was no federally recognized individual right to bear arms; there was a collective right. In other words, an individual that belonged to a militia could have one. Originally it was up to each state and city to regulate the guns within their jurisdiction, which meant that they were able to pass laws that prevented black or poor people from owning whatever gun they pleased. This prevented it from being a federally recognized right from its inception until 2008.

Court case after court case stated the reason it did not belong to the individual was to prevent black people from owning guns. Additionally, some of the legislation attempted by democrats in the 1990s would have prevented the very poor from owning guns. So now, everyone can own guns because of the individual right to bear arms. So, when you hear people on the right argue that the freedom to own guns is about rejecting tyranny and oppression, they are correct. It's not the only method by far; preventing us from owning guns so we can be oppressed is one of the methods. One last point to consider about this decision, the DC vs. Heller case did say that regulations could still be imposed. This means we now have the task of determining what limitations are needed.

This new interpretation and the allowance for limitations are why there have been so many recent arguments about what exactly is allowed. Because out of the nearly two and a half centuries of our country's existence, we only (relatively) recently changed a foundational right to our freedoms, so now we need to figure out what that means.

People are not trying to take away the freedom we've always had. Freedom has been expanded to include everyone, and now we're trying to determine the extent of this freedom we just received. That is a good thing. We have been expanding freedoms since our country was founded.

I hope this starts a conversation, so let's start with some of the questions up for discussion; while I have my opinions, I may not have the best ideas for the country. What happens to the gun ownership rights of convicted felons? What about violent offenders? Should people with a mental illness own guns? What about PTSD? How about ADD? If someone is feeling suicidal, should they keep their guns? Should they be suspended? What if someone is a domestic abuser but has not been convicted? Should the gun show loophole be closed? Does there need to be a list of registered gun owners? Why or why not?

Should we have statewide gun licenses like we do with cars? Would some licenses allow different types of weapons, like we do for motorcycles and large trucks? Would those licenses be able to cross state lines? Should we take a safety course for each level of license like we do for driving? Could those licenses serve as voter IDs?

The level of thoughtfulness and consideration that these answers require cannot be covered in a soundbite, which is all we ever hear in our media or amongst our political leaders. However, we can have these conversations around the dinner table. Then we can influence the conversations held in political institutions. We can help realize the changes that need to take place.

Who is trying to convince us that we cannot have a dialogue on gun rights and that everyone is coming for our guns? That's easy; they always say it and even have a whole TV station dedicated to their nonstop conspiracy theories. It's the NRA. They want us to be afraid and do not care about us or our rights.

In fact, since the Cincinnati Coup in 1977, the NRA has only cared about the interest of gun manufacturers. For those that do not know, the Coup was when they changed from an organization focused on hunting and conservation to a political movement. Unfortunately, the larger organization decided they were more interested in money from the gun manufacturers than in securing everyone's rights.

Before I go on, let me be clear, I'm talking about the organizational leadership itself, not the members of the NRA. Many members are still focused on responsible gun ownership, but we will get back to that.

At the time of this coup, they started arguing about the individual's right to bear arms, which led to the 2008 decision. Because this is an argument that has been going on for over 40 years, so many of us may feel like this has been a right we've had forever.

To demonstrate what I mean by the leadership not caring about responsible gun ownership, every time there's a mass shooting, they express concern about our rights being taken away and focus on selling more weapons. This is the strategy they came up with in response to the Columbine shootings. They may or may not pay lip service to the victims, but they always try to get us to purchase more guns. Notably, they are suspiciously silent when a black gun owner is killed by a police officer solely for legally owning a gun, as they did with Philando Castille.

Every time there's a Democrat on the ticket for a political office, they try to tell us that they're coming for our guns and our rights. However, every time there's a Democrat in office, our gun rights are not infringed. Quite the opposite, President Obama, who the NRA demonized, expanded gun rights. But because he wanted to discuss those rights, he was demonized. So this fear was generated to sell more guns, and it keeps working.

There are lots of other organizations that promote responsible gun safety without becoming political lobbyists. There are a wide variety of organizations out there that can teach people how to be responsible gun owners, some of which are tailored to subsets of the population, like those focused on Black or LGBTQ gun owners.

But for now, let's keep talking about those rights and how that's being done currently. First, the Second Amendment to the U.S. Constitution states, "A well-regulated Militia, being necessary to the security of a free State, the right of the people to keep and bear Arms, shall not be infringed." Each part of this amendment has been dissected for the original intent.

Some interpret the meaning of militia as the National Guard; some court cases interpreted it to also mean militias designed to abolish slave rebellions. So, to this point, almost from the conception of the amendment, it was not designed for the individual. But, again, going back to the beginning of this section, if everyone could own a gun, that means that free slaves could own them as well.

The current thought on this amendment is that it is for citizens to fight back against an oppressive government. But that was not how it was originally used to ensure that citizens could help suppress people for the state. States would allow militias to own guns to arrest escaping enslaved people but would not allow for freed blacks to have those same weapons.

If we genuinely want this to be a freedom that is allowed to everyone, then we need to ensure everyone's rights are protected. Currently, the loudest voice in politics concerning gun rights, the NRA, doesn't look out for all gun owners, and they historically haven't.

The gun owners they haven't defended have been murdered for defending their homes, having a gun safely stored in their car, or playing with a toy gun. The NRA is silent when they have a gun safely stored in their car and the police pull a gun on them.[1] Unfortunately, not just the leadership but many other gun owners are silent. In this case, silence is consenting for the state to murder those who lawfully own a gun.

The NRA is silent when they are a black teacher, have a gun, lawfully, in their car, and are shot by police. The NRA is very silent when black gun owners or black children playing with toys are shot. They have even supported laws that took away guns exclusively from black people.

More reprehensibly, they have said that we were under attack from black people and liberals, which excuses this violence against black gun owners. We are not under attack. We do not need to be more afraid of a black person with a gun than we should be of a white person with a gun. We all have a right to gun ownership. As you can tell, while I support our right to own guns, I do not like the NRA for their shallow hypocrisy that costs people their lives.

This behavior was shown again, as expected. Once a Democratic president was elected, memes started circulating that a well-armed populace needs to stand up to their oppressors. Meaning that the democratically elected government needed to be overthrown. However, these same people didn't share these memes when people of color protested police officers? There wasn't the suggestion that Native Americans needed to take up arms against the government and oil companies when those groups tried to take their land and poison their water supply?

Many people are getting frustrated with guns, and gun ownership, because they see constant news coverage of a new mass shooting on a frighteningly regular basis. Followed quickly by statements offering "thoughts and prayers" and statements that it is "too soon" to have a discussion about guns. A discussion that never comes.

We already talk to our kids about what to do when there is a shooter in their school. Nonwhite parents already talk to their children about how to avoid being murdered. Yet, far-right talk show hosts immediately start calling school shootings false flags and doxing survivors. Why is it okay for those conversations to continually take place but not one about responsible gun ownership?

Schools make children take active shooter drills, but when these shootings occur, the discourse is that this is not the time to discuss regulations. Or that we need to put more police in schools. There are already police in schools, and putting more of them in schools will not help. Besides, like in the case of the Columbine shooting, they are most likely not going to enter until after the shooting has stopped. Police are good at stopping a shooting before it starts, but once the shooting starts, it's usually one of the intended victims, like a student or teacher, that stops them.

If we are serious about ensuring our gun rights are maintained, then we need to have this conversation. Otherwise, gun ownership and their views will most likely continue to drop throughout the country. This means that if a conversation does not take place, then people will vote to have harsh restrictions. Because if we had to pick between a child and a gun, what would we pick?

Ok, back on topic, the point of this is to reinforce that gun ownership is something we can have in common with our fellow Americans. In fact, for those of you with friends that have not been shooting, I would recommend taking them. Let them know that if they want to relieve the stress, they should take a shotgun or semi-automatic rifle to the range. If they want to meditate, take them to a range where they can fire for 300 to 500 yards so they can focus on their breathing. If they want a combination, take them to shoot handguns.

This is something we can bond over. This is something we can have in common. The only people trying to convince us otherwise are literally trying to take our money or control our vote.

The biggest ask I could make is to stop thinking that people are coming for our guns. As I said, I know there are some proposals to license gun owners, but let us be honest, the likelihood of something like that passing is low. Plus, drivers' licenses didn't outlaw cars.

The second asks that I have to participate in the discussions on what the limits of this new freedom might become. I want us to participate in these conversations to ensure that whatever is enacted makes sense for everyone.

The third ask I have is that if we're going to stand up for the rights of some gun owners, we need to stand up for the rights of ALL gun owners. This freedom was expanded to allow all citizens the right to bear arms, and we need to continue to work towards the promise of our country.

The last is to bond with friends that like to go shooting simply, and for those that have never gone, invite them. If they do not see the need to have guns or have never fired one, then offer to take them to the range. Then, of course, make them split the cost of ammo. They'll probably have a good time, and you'll have more in common.

Back to the point about regulation, many people agree that the people, not the guns, need the regulation. Start the conversation there. Talk about the need to study gun violence. We have been prevented from having this conversation in the public arena for fear of what it may mean for gun sales and political contributions. These studies would show how guns are being used and misused. If guns are used defensively as much as people claim, then that would be good to know. But right now, there is a woeful lack of studies that lack a political agenda.

We have and continue to take many actions to ensure the safety of Americans. For example, we all regularly consent to take off our shoes before boarding an airplane because one idiot attempted to use a shoe bomb. We lock up tide pods because other idiots decided they would be a tasty treat. For any of us to get Sudafed at the store, we have to show our driver's license, and it has to be checked against a database because someone might be able to make drugs with it. So we have already taken drastic actions in our society to deal with minor problems, and I can see that people are concerned that we will take drastic action against guns. But that doesn't mean we should continue to do nothing that's not been working.

Look at the way a different industry is regulated, cars. In the U.S., we can buy a crazy variety of vehicles, some of which are custom-built for specific purposes. Some of them, like a Lamborghini, are overkill in the states, as there is nowhere for them to cut loose, but they are still allowed. So, what do we do? We ensure that people are trained to safely operate a vehicle and give them a license for specific classes of vehicles. Then, if they are ever unsafe or a danger to themselves, their families, or the community, we take their cars away.

So how about the same with guns? Again, it does say regulated militia, and even in the 2008 decision, the Supreme Court stated that regulations could still be imposed. Many gun owners, myself included, are worried that if this toxic environment continues, we as a country will get to the point where we become anti-gun.

No one wants bad guys to have guns. We want to lower the number of suicides in the U.S. We want gun owners to have some level of safety training.

Now onto those that may not be comfortable with guns or gun ownership at all. Let us start with the obvious; there are a lot of fantastic reasons to own a gun. I spoke about a few of the above, but one that is brought up all the time and everyone seems to ignore is self-defense. Why?

Because the police are not legally required to protect you. That's right, court case after court case states that they are not legally required to protect you. This is not disparaging of the police. I agree with those decisions, and it makes sense once you know the reasoning.

As a member of the military, the first thing I signed up to do was to fight the enemies of the United States; everything else was secondary. Police sign up to serve their community, which does include protection, but we cannot legally require them to sacrifice their lives to do something, even protect us.

This means that the right to self-defense falls solely upon us. Just us. No one else is required to come and save us. Think about that for a second. Think about all the cases we have read about police not going into a dangerous and unknown situation. Of course, some of us would have gone into a dangerous situation to protect others, but holding someone legally responsible if they do is not the right answer.

That's why one of the primary reasons to own a gun is to defend our homes and families. That is one of the reasons I own guns. Plus, guns of all types have been used defensively in numerous cases.

Unfortunately, the exact numbers around this are inconsistent. Some point out the problem with reporting incidents that did work but were not reported or cases that did not occur because there was a weapon present. That's part of the reason I brought up the issue of studying gun usage.

Hunting is another great reason to have a gun. Although, frankly, while I may be terrible at hunting, those are more armed nature walks for me than they are actually hunting expeditions. Many people are very good at it, or at least good enough to feed their families all year round.

I know several people that can stock their freezers with meat for most of the year from one hunting season. This obviously saves them a lot of money throughout the year. Hunting also has a lot of benefits for maintaining healthy populations of animals and preserving the environment.

But what about "military-style" rifles? I know that some people like to point out that there is no reason to own those types of weapons. To which I ask, why not? Yes, those weapons are primarily used to kill people, or materials, hence the "military" part, but why should that prevent people from owning them?

To some people, they are a reminder of the weapons that they used in the military. They know how to use them, and they like them. They are fun to shoot. Some people like to cosplay like they were in the military, and I cannot judge someone for liking cosplay. Some people just like to own and shoot them. Plus, some of them are really good at self-defense and hunting.

As I alluded to before, there is research to show that the gun owner, not the gun, needs to be focused on when discussing defensive use. These "military-style" weapons have been used by people defending their families as well as other types of guns.

But what about things like school shootings? What about mass shootings? There are far too many of those. Fortunately, despite the debates we see in our media, most of us in the U.S. agree on ways to limit these events.

Polling indicates that most people are in support of closing loopholes that allow people to purchase these weapons without background checks. Plus, people want to ensure that criminals do not own guns. But what about mental illness? What kinds of mental illness? ADD? PTSD? How severe?

One of the reasons I repeated PTSD is because a lot of former military members have PTSD, and they own guns. Not all PTSD makes people violent; many of us know people who live with PTSD from a traumatic event, but that does not make them incapable of living.

My first ask for those who don't own guns is understanding that there are legitimate reasons to own guns. All types of them. If you live in a rural environment, like I do, gun ownership makes a lot of sense.

Also, do not be afraid of guns outright; they are a tool, a tool used for killing, yes, but a tool, nonetheless. If you want to learn more about them, talk to someone who owns one. If you want to buy one for self-defense, talk to someone about describing your needs and environment.

Learning how to use a firearm safely is very important, and while I have not hidden my opinions about the larger NRA organization, their gun safety classes are great. They were originally a hunting and gun safety group, and if they offer a class in your area, I would recommend taking it. Their local organizations will help ensure you get the training and knowledge you need to operate a gun safely and competently.

Speaking to someone at a gun store about your needs is a good way to get a gun that fits your needs and style. For those that don't know, the combination of guns and ammunition is very important when purchasing. Buying a gun is like buying a car; one size does not fit all, and many options can change the performance. Again, like a car, it takes a lot of training to become comfortable using it. Also (most) gun dealers take their role seriously, and they won't force a sale upon someone or make an inappropriate sale.

How about we end this with an ask for all of us. We all agree on the need to save lives and keep one another safe. In poll after poll, we have all agreed that waiting periods for purchases and background checks are good. They help to reduce the number of suicides and, in some cases, would prevent some of our mass shootings.

The next time we are at the range together, we can talk about writing and calling our representatives to get those things enacted. Also, one last time because I see it so often in my social media feed, no one is coming for our guns. But, again, if we do not do something constructive about this topic, I worry that we are poisoning the well regarding gun ownership.

---

1. Serwer, Adam. "The NRA's Catch-22 for Black Men Shot by Police", The Atlantic, September 13, 2018, https://www.theatlantic.com/ideas/archive/2018/09/the-nras-catch-22-for-black-men-shot-by-police/570124/.

Chapter Nineteen

We Need to Fix Policing

The state of policing in the U.S. is broken. We ask too much of them. We train them inappropriately to handle the situations being asked of them. We disproportionately arm them for their taskings. As a result, too many of us are dying. We need to fix this.

Like the last section, people are dying. Both Police officers and the citizens they serve. We need to fix this because it is unsustainable. We need to recognize that the vast majority of police join up to serve communities, and we need the police to remember that they are public servants.

Here is one of those sections where I do not think either side has the moral high ground. During the summer of 2020 protests, lots of liberals were saying, "All Cops Are Bastards." Then during the January 6th, 2021, insurrection at the capitol, while carrying the U.S. and "Blue" lives matter flags, cops were beaten, one of which with an actual U.S. flag. Both sides use the police as a political tool and sympathize with them when they are on the opposite side of the argument.

Let's start with the ask of treating cops better, across the board, in many ways. Of course, all of us need to treat them better. But, they are neither a monolith nor a token we can hold up to feign our support.

For those worried that I am starting off asking for better treatment of the police, just know that I am not writing this for them. I am writing this as a way for all of us to improve our community, of which they are a part. We will cover ways to help the police better engage with communities and how there needs to be a perspective shift. One that has been growing and needs to continue.

Let's start with a couple of examples of how the current state of policing in the U.S. is dangerous to both the police and the population being served. The first incident involved police aggressively pulling a military member out of their car and arresting them before releasing them without being charged. The military member had pulled over into a well-lit area for everyone's protection. The police were very angry and disrespectful towards the service member for not immediately complying with all their requests. They had their weapons drawn and threatened to shoot him on several occasions. One of the officers was fired for this behavior. The second was a police officer being murdered at a traffic stop. The police officer had pulled over a vehicle, and the person stepped out with an AR-15 and murdered him.

The current state of policing in the U.S. is dangerous to both the police and the citizens. I know that a lot of people want to fix this issue, police included, and we need to start working on solutions so we can save one another.

Also, before we start going down this path, I think it is important to recognize that while we are only addressing the state of policing in the U.S., as recent history has shown us, we are not unique in having to repair the relationship between the people being served and those tasked with their protection. On the plus side, we seem to be actively interested in having these conversations and improving this relationship.

Let's start with the police. When someone signs up to help their community, they sign up to help their community, not to be oppressive bullies. They want to protect and help.

Are there bad cops? Yes. Are there bad people in any job? Yes. Should cops, and other people placed in a position of public trust, be held to a higher standard? Yes.

Do we place a lot of disparate responsibilities upon the police without providing the resources to perform those tasks, not to mention the pay adequately? Yes. Do we already do that with other positions with a public trust? Again, yes. We already hold nurses, teachers, and members of the military to a higher standard. It is time to hold the police to one as well.

Many ideas that I will bring up on improving this situation are taken from community activists and police officers. Oddly enough, in many ways, they say the same thing. They both have similar ideas to fix the problems; now, we just need to help make it happen.

Speaking of the problem with how policing is framed is how it is portrayed in our media, lots of the counter-protests to the Black Lives Matter movement used the refrain that "Blue Lives Matter" against the movement. The largest problem with using this as a counter-argument is that the conversation is now framed as "Blacks vs. Cops," which is intentionally harmful to both communities.

This framing makes it sound like the police must fight black people or that they are under siege by the black community. Unfortunately, this mindset has led to several false comparisons. First off, blacks may like to kill cops. The second is that black cops were somehow "race traitors." How absurd are either of those arguments?

Just as a thought exercise, considering how many black police chiefs came out to talk to the public during the protests, do you think they want to hurt the black community? Do you think they took those jobs to be oppressive? Do you think these chiefs want to oppress their own communities? The overwhelming majority of police want to make things better. They want to connect to the populations that they serve.

Am I saying there is not a problem? No. There is a problem with accountability. There is a problem with training. There is a problem with the equipment. These are all very apparent.

These are also the same problems that some activists and police members point out as needing to be resolved. Yet, these are the topics that they both agree upon. Therefore, it is something that we could both fight to improve.

The first topic is holding people accountable for their actions. Holding public figures accountable for their actions is nothing new. We have done it for the military, doctors, intelligence agencies, nurses, and more. Increasing accountability and transparency has always done wonders in increasing public trust in those organizations. This works for everyone, we want to trust the police, and they want us to trust them. That will make our communities safer.

How about we put this another way. For a long time, people in the medical profession had an enormous amount of leeway with how they treated people and the care that they showed them. However, this resulted in many people dying or receiving poor treatment and, in some cases, medical experimentation.

Then we decided that they should be held accountable for their actions and do things like wash their hands and not leave medical devices inside people after an operation, or not give communities diseases to see their effects. Or that they should give their patients the right medications at the right times. Since implementing these changes, we have had a vastly improved medical system that has focused a lot on patient care.

In fact, it is so exact that if a medical professional makes one error in distributing medication, they can lose their jobs.

Think about that, how many jobs are you allowed to do a mistake in without fear of completely losing your job? Well, a good reason is allowed; if a medical professional makes a mistake, someone could die. Many people did before these rules were put into effect.

Or how about we look at a profession in which too many police departments are trying to emulate, the military. Before we go down this rabbit hole, we need to clarify that the military and the police have very different mission sets that we should never get confused about. The military serves its communities by defending them from the enemies of the state. The police serve by protecting the communities they are a part of, which the military is protecting. The military can become an occupying force; the police should never be.

Ok, so off down the rabbit hole. We have a volunteer military force, which has always trained to have each other's back, whether in the same branch or another. We know that we are going to be put in harm's way and that we will be in dangerous situations. However, we must always follow the Uniform Code of Military Justice (UCMJ). If you violate this code, you lose your rank and go to prison.

How does this apply to policing? There are currently too many examples of a lack of accountability within police departments. It's even sadder when we read stories about good police officers that are fired for trying to hold bad police officers accountable.

The main impediment to resolving this issue is police unions. These unions, like other unions, are good at taking care of their people. But this level of care should not be allowed to shield people that have committed crimes.

Like we will discuss as it applies to teachers, we place a lot of responsibilities upon people in the public trust without comparable pay. In my experience, as a part of the military, we send 18-year-olds to foreign countries and expect them to serve as ambassadors, community leaders, technicians, and mechanics, and, when needed, violent fighters. These are not separate examples for multiple 18-year-olds; this is the example of one day in that person's life in the field.

Likewise, we expect our police to track murderers and rapists, handle traffic accidents, solve domestic disputes, be there when people have mental health issues (suicidal or self-harm tendencies, hallucinations), deal with the homeless, and more. But, again, this is in one day for the same officer. Plus, since I have never been a cop, I am sure I missed something.

Another similarity between police and teachers, besides the high workloads, low pay, and impossibly high standards, is the fact that they are in unions. Police and teachers' unions can be a good thing as long as they are doing the right thing by caring for and protecting their members. However, if they allow a "bad egg," to borrow a euphemism, to stay, they undermine all their good work. Not just some, but all of it.

What would we think if a teacher rapes their students and the union demands they keep their job? Likewise, if a police officer rapes or murders someone, why should they be allowed to keep their job.

We all agree that teachers who rape students should get arrested. We should all agree that police officers who murder someone should be arrested and not protected by their unions. As it would make every teacher in a union look bad if they stood by the rapist, it makes police unions look bad by not holding their own members accountable.

So how do we fix the problem of accountability? Start with local levels, and find out how your local departments handle accountability. Then, find out what can be done to improve that accountability. There are police unions that prevent accountability in many cases, but they need to be held responsible for those actions. There is a lot of good that comes from unions, but unfortunately, there can be a lot of bad that can come from them. This is something that we can all work on to improve.

There can be huge resistance to change in this scenario. The medical professions and the military were, and are, resistant to change. However, the changes to the military and medical professions not only improved those professions but saved many lives; the same is true for police. Holding it more accountable will do a lot to save lives, not just of the population being served but the police officers themselves.

Next, let's look at how they are trained. There are two disparate schools of thought about training a police officer as a warrior or guardian. One, the warrior, is in a constant state of aggression and never at peace. This type of attitude automatically puts them in conflict with the population they are supposed to be serving. The other, the guardian, is a public servant who builds relationships and trust within the community they serve.

Are you a sheep? Are the police members of the community? Should every encounter with a police officer be escalated to the point of violence? I hope that we all agree on the answers to this.

In many of the warrior training, they are told they are always warriors and that the people are sheep. Also, if they are told that they are a warrior, every encounter is naturally a conflict and must be escalated. Being trained to think they are warriors puts them opposed to the communities they are supposed to serve. If everything is an adversarial relationship, does that make an interaction safer or more dangerous? I ask this in terms of both the police and the citizens.

A warrior mindset allows police to treat a senior citizen with dementia as a threat. This mindset allows them to beat an elderly confused woman until they break her body. This mindset encourages them to go back to the police station and openly brag about the violence. If everyone is a threat, it makes sense to beat them and cheer your victory in battle even though your opponent was a lost older woman in need of help.

Are our local police trained to be servants of the population? When we need to call them, do we want the police to start with an adversarial relationship with us, or do we need their help? If we need their help, do we want them to come in escalating the situation? I have called the police countless times over the years to help resolve numerous situations, and I have had the fortune of working with police members of the community who were always focused on providing a service to the community.

This warrior mindset is dangerous to the police and the communities they serve. This mindset instantly puts them into conflict with their community and naturally escalates any encounter toward violence.

Conversely, there is the guardian mindset. This mindset reinforces that the police are members of the community. This mindset ensures that they treat the people needing their help with respect. Of course, this doesn't mean they can't be violent when the time comes, but it does make them more prone to deescalate a situation. With a guardian mindset, the police can respond to a crisis situation and ensure everyone safely goes home or to jail.

What can we do? We can find out how the local departments are trained. Find out what kind of mindset they have. Spoiler alert, if your local law enforcement has a good relationship with the community, they are guardians. Find out if they are trained in de-escalation techniques. Find out what training they receive and what they might need. Go to board meetings to talk about budgets. Involvement is rarely glamorous, but it gets results.

Now let's move on to talking about funding. This is where those aforementioned meetings come in handy. Because simply removing funding from the police while leaving the same level of responsibility, or just abolishing the police, can set our communities up for failure. Paying attention to the responsibilities we ask of them in our communities and the problems we are facing in those respective communities will help us find what is appropriate for where we live. If we divest them of responsibilities that should never have been given to them and move the funding to more appropriate agencies, then that is something that most people can support. In some areas, there may need to be an increased police presence. This is where it comes down to each community and why we all need to get involved.

As we spoke about earlier, many disparate responsibilities are being placed upon police officers within our community. They are being asked to solve crimes, handle traffic accidents, monitor schools, resolve domestic disputes, and much more. Defunding them alone would not solve the problems we are asking them to address.

Therefore, we all need to look at what our community needs. Does it need more parks? Does it need more teachers? Does it need road maintenance? Does it need more after-school programs? Does it need more substance abuse counsellors? All our communities have different needs. Sending the police to handle all of them cannot work because many of the problems in our community cannot be fixed by arresting someone or writing a ticket.

A lot of the problems in our communities take hard work and time. So, look at our communities, and see what is needed. As we discussed in the section on taxes, budgets are a reflection of priorities and morals. What our community spends money on, they find important.

Go to the local government meetings. Ask questions. Speak about your needs. Listen to other people speak about theirs. Parts of your community may need more police, some less. There is no universal answer for this, but help your elected officials make better decisions.

Lastly, let's talk about equipment. Currently, the police have tremendous leeway in what they are allowed to purchase, and it makes sense as to why. After the terrorist attacks on September 11, many people felt afraid, for a good reason, and they wanted to feel protected.

Therefore, the police were given the military equipment and weapons to fight terrorists. Two federal programs allow police departments, including university departments, to purchase military equipment at all levels. The 1033 program allows the federal government to transfer military equipment to these departments. The 1122 program allows local police departments to purchase military equipment at the same discount as the military.

Plus, with the wars the U.S. was fighting, there was a lot of equipment leftover which police departments could acquire. Equipment like Mine Resistant Ambush Protected (MRAP) vehicles. Now, for those who do not know, these are wonderful vehicles to use in a combat environment. They do a phenomenal job of protecting people from every angle and enabling troops to enter a dangerous and hostile environment and get out safely. As a piece of military hardware, they are great, to the point where one person said that even if we drove them all into the ocean when we were done in Iraq, they were worth the investment because of the lives saved.

My question is, why does any police force need that level of protection? Is your local police force an occupying force? Do they view us as a threat? How do we want our police force to relate to the community they serve? Now, I picked on the MRAP because I love them. But how many other pieces of military equipment do our local police agencies need?

Let us work together and make policing better for everyone, both the police and the population they serve. Get involved locally and find out about accountability. Find out how accountability is handled. Is it through the local prosecutors that have to work with the police and are therefore inclined not to charge them with a crime?

Find out if they are encouraged, or in some cases discouraged, to live with the populations that they serve. See how they handle raids and no-knock warrants, which are very dangerous to the cops and the population they serve and are not needed in most cases. Find a way to help distribute their workload in a way that makes sense and lets them do the job that we need them to do and want to perform. Find a way to make sure they get the necessary training and support to do the tasks that your community needs them to perform. Doing these things will make everyone's lives easier and safer, both the police and the population they serve.

Chapter Twenty

Simple Prison Reforms

What is the point of prison? More specifically, what is the role of prison within our society? What do we want it to do for us? Who should go to prison? What crimes require prison time? How do we want prisons to treat the people inside of them? What kind of people do we want to come out of them and back into our society?

What do we want prison to do? Do we want them to punish someone solely, or do we want them to reform them? Do we want some combination of the two? Does our answer change upon the type of crime committed? These questions will help us determine the type of people that will emerge from our prison systems.

Nearly 1% of our population is currently incarcerated, which is the largest percentage of incarcerated people in the world. Numerically we house one-fifth of the world's prisoners. Dictatorships have a much smaller percentage. Is this because we are so uncivilized that we need many of us in prison, or is there another reason?

How about we start with the easy stuff? I think we can all agree that violent offenders need to be in prison. If someone is responsible for a violent crime, I do not think anyone is on the side of continuing to allow them to remain in society, especially without being reformed.

But what do we want them to be like when they have served their time? Should they be allowed to find housing? Should they be allowed to find a job? If we say no to either of those, why? They have served their time and suffered the consequences.

Do we want to remain a country that perpetually punishes people once they have done their time or made amends? When we have gotten in trouble, were we continually punished for that one act, or were we allowed to make amends? Once they have served their time, their punishment is legally over; therefore, we should stop punishing them.

But that is not what happens. We have a bad habit of marking people who have been convicted for the rest of their lives, making it harder for them to find housing and employment. This makes it much harder for them to reenter society and become a productive member. If we do not help them become productive members, then we are casting them aside, continually excluding them.

If we do not teach them how to live and function within our society, how can they be expected to function properly? If we do not give them a trade to learn, what should they do when they get out? If we do not set people up for success, we are setting them up for failure.

Now onto the more difficult part, who should go to prison? Do we want to send everyone that commits a crime? What about minor crimes like drug possession? What if you got caught smoking a joint? How many people do you know have ever smoked a joint? How many of us drank alcohol underage? Should all of us go to prison? Most of us think that we probably should not.

Unfortunately, though, we currently send many people to prison for simple drug usage. Why? What are we, as a society, trying to say about this? Additionally, if we are saying that simple drug usage, like smoking a joint, is something worthy of prison, we are telling the police that it is worthy of their time. Is that something they should be concerned with, or do we want police focused on more important things?

Since this is in the section of the book that I think we agree upon and can do the most about, how about, we get to that part. As I am sure most of us have heard, an ounce of prevention is worth a pound of cure. Well, in nearly half of our states, the amount of money we spend per inmate is 24 thousand dollars more than we spend per student. How about we fix that? Not by reducing the money to care for prisoners, but by decreasing the number of people in prison so that we can increase the amount we spend on children, and our environments, like public parks and libraries. We easily find that much money to put people in prison, but how do we have so much trouble finding money to keep them out?

What are some things that we can do to fix this issue? The below ideas are things that many of us, regardless of political ideology, can agree upon. So, let's work on getting our politicians to enact these things.

First, we can change the laws to reduce the number of people who go to prison. If they are a non-violent offender, why should we even send them? If they have a drug habit, we should treat their addiction, so they do not go back to using. This would not only help the user but would reduce the tax burden on the population because treating a drug user instead of sending them to prison would save the taxpayer 20 thousand dollars per user. Additionally, this reduces the workload on police officers of having to arrest people for simple drug use or possession.

Second, we could get rid of private prisons. These systems allow corporations to get rich off tax dollars by ensuring that people remain imprisoned. In fact, these private prisons have written their contracts to ensure that they get the maximum amount of tax revenue by having their contracts state that if not enough people get sent to the prison (total occupancy), then they get to charge the state an additional fee. This means the state is actively incentivized to send people to prison. Is that how we want to spend our tax dollars?

While these are policies that most of us agree upon, they are policies that most politicians do not want to enact. Many of the problems that we currently have with our policing and prison system were put in place by Senator Biden, who now, as president, is not eager to overturn them. We can work to get rid of mandatory minimum sentencing and egregious rules, like the "3 strikes" rule, that sends nonviolent people to prison for the rest of their lives. There is far more than this that we can do to reform our system. But these actions would move it towards providing actual justice.

Chapter Twenty-One

We Have Fixed the Environment Before; We Can Do It Again

Back in the 1970s, a problem was identified in numerous places around the world. Lots of trees and plants were dying. The soil was becoming more acidic, and structures were being slowly destroyed. But we were convinced not to believe the evidence presented, even when we could see the results. Then, when the evidence was strong enough to see the results with our eyes, we were told that fixing the problem would destroy the economy. So, we fixed it anyway, and we got stronger economically.

When they first observed the trees and plants dying in the 1970s, scientists brought their findings to the public and proposed methods to halt these effects. Politicians, at the behest of their donors, said that the scientists' data was either incomplete or wrong and that they needed to go back and look at the problem further. The politicians took it a step further and said that if any action was taken to address this issue, the economy would collapse, and people would lose their jobs.

To the surprise of no one, the problem continued to get worse, with forests dying and infrastructure beginning to crumble. Finally, in the early 1980s, and after increasing international pressure, politicians could no longer deny the damage being done to the environment.

Once the politicians were forced into action, the problem was solved in a relatively short amount of time. The solution to the problem required businesses to halt the production of chemicals that polluted the environment. The regulations were put in place so businesses could adjust without taking on an unreasonable burden.

The problem that I have been writing about was acid rain. Who remembers that? Most people who were alive during that time barely remember this being a problem despite the concerted global effort and weather advisories.

Several countries used different methods to address the problem, but the U.S. used Cap and Trade to resolve this issue and keep businesses competitive. This is why we hear this method being discussed to resolve our current climate-related problems. Cap and Trade is a method that allows businesses to work together on solving the problem while remaining financially competitive. Granted, it also forces them to take responsibility for their actions and clean up their messes.

Also, as you will notice, the global economy did not collapse in solving this problem, and businesses were allowed to thrive. In fact, the 1980s and 1990s were known for their economic prosperity. This means another spoiler alert is due; solving our current crisis will not wreck our economy if we do it right.

In fact, a lot of the steps we've taken have created new and thriving parts of our economy.

With that in mind, we are going to move on to the current climate change crisis. After having a few conversations and doing some more research, I am amazed at the network of lies surrounding this topic, some of which have been used to stop us from cleaning up any environmental mess. To be fair, I am certain that I have not found all of them, but it does clarify one thing: I can understand why there is so much confusion and lack of coordination on this topic. Unfortunately, these lies are a feature of the conversation, not a bug. If we all do not know what's going on, we cannot identify the problem, much less do anything to fix the issue.

That's the reason for the lies surrounding this issue. When we agree on the facts, we move forward and take action. But if we can be convinced that there is no problem, or if the discussion gets poisoned enough, then no movement takes hold, and no action gets taken. We have all worked together to solve past problems, and we can work together to solve this one.

In my lifetime, we have changed the environment at least five times, but we only argue about one of them. We caused the problem that resulted in acid rain, and then we fixed it. We then created a hole in the ozone layer and fixed that. We only seem to be stuck on solving climate change.

As I am not that old, many of you may also remember these things. Older generations probably remember many regional environmental problems, such as rivers so polluted that they caught on fire regularly. Notice that these problems are not there now. We came together and fixed them. We did it quickly, and we did it in a way that did not destroy our economy. Additionally, the problem of leaded gasoline polluted the environment and poisoned the population on a global scale. But we switched to unleaded again without destroying our economy.

The only one of the issues that we seem to be arguing about is the current most pressing matter of climate change. On this issue, many of us have been lied to so much about the issue that we cannot recognize the problem, again, which is the point. If we can't recognize the problem, we are not going to do anything about it. This makes sense because if we all saw the problem, we could do amazing things to fix it. Like we have done before.

Let's start with some obvious things; climate change is happening. Scientists working for coal companies have known about it since the 1960s, and the oil and gas companies have known about it since the 1970s. This led to these industries making a concerted effort to say it was not real or to undermine the science. This is not a conspiracy theory; they publicly said this in 2014. The lie that climate change wasn't real started over 60 years ago. This is not a political statement; as some people like to say, facts do not care about feelings. The disagreement should be about how to address the problem, not whether the problem exists.

To be fair to those that still doubt this is happening, I would like to give some credit to a couple of massive lies that have circulated around this discussion. One of which is the fear-mongering during the 1970s and 1980s that there was going to be an upcoming ice age. Time and Newsweek both reported on that. Next is the shift to using the term climate change compared to global warming. This was done by a Republican strategist, Frank Luntz, to confuse the issue and make it partisan. Therefore, those on team Republican could be against climate action because those on team Democrat were in favor of fixing the climate. Since this, Luntz has come forward and said that this was a mistake and has damaged efforts to fix the problem.

This means that lies have become so pervasive that it's hard to believe in what is real. I get why this can confuse so many people about what is happening. There has been such a tangle of lies that it's hard to believe what's real. Unfortunately, like environmental issues of the past, we have entered the phase where we have begun to feel the effects of climate change.

While directly seeing these effects should help us see through the lies like it did with acid rain and leaded gasoline, it also means that we have crossed the threshold of avoiding those effects. So, let's start talking about what we need to do in order to fix the problem. Because there are many options before us, we need to take a varied approach to fix the issue before we start though we need to acknowledge that no option is perfect and that waiting for the perfect solution will just worsen the problem.

Think about it this way, if someone is in a dangerous situation and they need to get out, should they stay there until everything is perfect for them to get out? Should they stay in an abusive relationship because there is no other home for them to go to? Should they endure pain because there is no perfect alternative standing by? No, there are options that people have to get out of a dangerous situation.

Our current climate crisis is like that. The world heavily relies upon energy sources that are massive polluters. But switching our reliance on energy that doesn't pollute is more technologically feasible than ever. Unfortunately, we either lacked the political will or simply the focus on getting the job done.

We can fix this problem, and the U.S. must be the world leader in this manner. Because if anyone else was going to lead, they would have, and we can't wait for someone else to step up. The world's second-largest economy, China, can't even maintain clean air in its capital city and is determined to open more coal power plants across the country. Australia goes between fire and floods while its government denies climate change, so their politicians can get rich from exporting fossil fuels. Germany is closing their nuclear power plants and opening more coal power plants. The other countries that could have led are making the situation worse. We can show the world how to successfully shift energy sources while maintaining a strong economy and employment.

Let's start off by talking about nuclear energy. There are a lot of people that are adamantly opposed to this form of energy, but frankly, it is the greenest form of energy available to us until fusion power becomes a reality. The biggest impediment to this, though, is its negative connotation with nuclear weapons and waste. But politically, there is no will to implement this because while we are needlessly scared of it, it's far harder to get as rich off its use.

Are there concerns about nuclear energy that there is toxic waste? Well, that can be addressed; there are ways to help prevent that. Plus, most waste, like biological waste from hospitals, is things like gloves and outerwear. Things that aren't truly radioactive but can't be thrown in the regular trash. With the spent fuel rods, we already have solutions for disposing of those safely and responsibly that doesn't harm the planet.

Additionally, if the concerns about nuclear energy are that it may cause a smaller, controllable level of pollution, I have bad news about the current state of our energy producers. In fact, if the greatest concern about nuclear power plants is the radiation, then we should switch to nuclear power plants because coal power plants emit over 100 times more radiation than nuclear power plants. That doesn't include all of the other waste from a coal power plant.

Are the concerns about the level of deaths that may occur from an accident in a nuclear incident? That is why Germany and Japan switch from nuclear power to coal power, so how about we look at the numbers. The death from all causes per terawatt hour for nuclear power is 90. Solar energy is at 440 deaths. On the other hand, coal is at a whopping 100,000 deaths per terawatt hour. So, if we are looking at saving lives, then nuclear is the safest. Think about it this way; planes are vastly safer for people than cars, yet when there is a problem on a plane, everyone knows about it. The same applies to nuclear energy.

Do you know how many people died in the Fukushima reactor? One. More people died from evacuating, and many more died from the earthquake and tsunami that caused damage to the plant. But one person died. So, preventing human deaths and pollution cannot be the reason to oppose nuclear power, but I understand it can be scary. It's hard to imagine a nuclear power plant as safe, especially since many of us grew up watching Homer Simpson work as the person responsible for nuclear power plant safety.

Going back to the coal and oil industries, they knew back in the 1950s that nuclear power could replace their industries, which started a concerted effort on their part to convince us that nuclear was dangerous and that all the waste produced would be put into glowing barrels that leaked into our water supply. To this day, the oil and gas industries still give a lot of funding to anti-nuclear organizations to ensure that any expansion of this energy source is hindered or even reversed.

As a species, we demand more energy, and we need to ensure that the energy is clean. As such, we need to incorporate nuclear energy into the equation. Even if it is temporary, even if there is a better solution somewhere in the future, we need something that will not actively destroy the planet we live upon. We should have started building more nuclear power plants in the middle of the last century. Or we could have started when we first embraced climate change as an issue in the 1990s. But it's not too late to start now. This is a technology we can use now, proven safe even when hit with the worst environmental disasters.

In fact, there is a way to continue using nuclear power without the fear of meltdown or toxic waste. We could invest in reactors that use Thorium. We've researched this technology before but stopped because we couldn't make nuclear weapons out of it. Plus, it's easier to mine. This technology would require more research, but it's closer than fusion.

Let's reiterate a few ludicrous things. First, coal and oil companies, which have vast experience with mining, and at their core, deal with energy, have known since the middle of the last century that there is better technology out there that requires experienced miners to excavate and solves our energy crisis. On top of that, they've known for almost half a century that their industries are making the planet untenable for human survival. But instead of using this foresight to refocus their businesses and figure out a way to profit from this new future, they decided that it made more business sense to spend millions, possibly billions creating a false narrative and paying politicians to keep making policies that benefit their outdated model for providing energy.

Honestly, that is the point that perplexes me the most. How much cheaper would it have been for them to research alternate energy sources and be the world leader in those fields? It is like a horse and carriage seller accidentally inventing the car 50 years before anyone else. Instead of switching business models or even planning for the future, they try to convince everyone that cars are evil. If these companies had started the transition at the time, they would have been viewed as heroes, had a tremendous leg up on all of their competitors, and had an extremely loyal customer base. They would have been Tesla 50 years before Tesla existed.

To be fair, though, electric cars have been around since before the civil war. That's right, electric cars have been around longer than gas-powered cars, since before the civil war. But we are just now starting to use them and act like they are a brand-new invention. To be fair, the energy storage issue is new.

But these points prove that continuing to allow the "free market" and "capitalism" to fix the problem is foolish. These industries had nearly 70 years to adjust and fix the problem, and they still are fighting it. Instead, they lied to us about solutions and, as we will discuss later, who is to blame. That doesn't mean they don't deserve a seat at the table moving forward, but they have to earn it.

Here should be where those on the right and left should be having a discussion. How do we solve the problem? What should be done? How do we keep our economy going strong while facing an existential crisis? The last time we did this, we used a "Cap and Trade" model to address the issue. Would it be better to use a straight tax on carbon usage?

It's not the first time we've come together to address an existential crisis; it probably won't be the last. So here is where I would challenge all of us to elect officials who want to work on solving climate change, whether on the left or right. The time for denial has long passed. We must ensure that we can address this issue from multiple perspectives, but we can't ignore it.

In addition to the lies and manipulation we discussed above, there are the usual delaying tactics being done with any movement forward. The same arguments that were used against addressing the hole in the ozone, or any other environmental problem that we have had to deal with, it'll cost jobs, it's bad for business, and there's no way it can be done and keep competitive. Polluters have used these arguments for decades, but they should not prevent action while they are concerned. There have been numerous cases where we have forced polluters to take responsibility for their actions that have enabled them to stay in business. Granted, there have been some cases where that responsibility has put them out of business, but they should still be held accountable for their damage.

Since we have already entered the phase where we have started to experience the repercussions of our inaction on climate change, we should know what further implications there will be for the country. However, there have been far better-written papers about what will happen, so that I will make a couple of overly simplistic points. Mainly, if we do nothing, the economic impact will be far worse than if we start tackling the problem. Trillions of dollars will need to be spent on the damage alone, and if we do nothing worldwide, GDP could drop by at least 20%. Estimates about the cost of climate change in the U.S. in 2020 alone are around hundreds of billions of dollars and hundreds of thousands of deaths from the severe weather events and the damage they caused. Then all the health-related problems result from the pollution and the aforementioned extreme events.

On the bright side, working to fix the problem has already enabled massive scientific development and job growth. In addition, the work that has already been done has led to many jobs being created. Most notably is the difference between the coal and solar industries. For decades, due to increased safety and automation, coal jobs have been decreasing. In contrast, due to decreased costs, solar jobs have been drastically increasing. While we should continue this trend, we need to ensure that the communities that were centered on coal mining have a future as well. They need it.

Speaking of coal mining communities. They should not be forgotten. The people there helped to power our civilization for a long time, and we can't forget them because their company owners were short-sighted. Therefore, we need to encourage politicians to implement policies that allow them to get opportunities that fit the current technology. Be understanding and compassionate to your neighbors. We all want people to have jobs; fixing the environment and stimulating the economy are not mutually exclusive.

I am focusing so much attention on corporations right now and why we need to find ways to encourage them to fix the problem because there are only 100 companies worldwide that account for about 71% of greenhouse gas emissions. Therefore, while we may be taking individual actions that contribute to making the world cleaner, no one of us can fix the damage continually being done by these companies. So, if some of us cannot make some of the recommendations I make in this chapter, don't feel guilty. We all must function in this society, but we can all work to make it better.

Fixing the environment is a massive problem. It is quite literally an existential one and will require massive effort to fix. Moreover, some of the things that will be needed to fix this issue will be hated by some because some of the solutions will keep energy companies rich and operating, even as they switch business models.

Here I want to take a few minutes and talk about one of the themes of this book, the ability to look at something from a different perspective and change your mind. When I was a kid, the Exxon Valdez crashed in Alaska, causing a lot of environmental damage, and long story short, I swore that I would never go to that gas station again. With the anger that only comes with adolescence, I swore that if we ran out of gas near one, I would push it to the next gas station.

Now, while it never came to that, how would that young man feel about the fact that I bought stock in that same company? Well, he would be angry at first, but the anger he felt was about the damage that the company had done to the environment. However, now that I had bought that stock, I did something that he could never imagine. As a stockholder, I vote during their annual stockholder meeting, and several of the things I voted on were their environmental policies and how they will address climate change. Now granted, I do not have much of a vote, but many other people were voting along the same lines and were interested in the same topics. This resulted in several people being elected to their board that are interested in cleaning up the environment. Therefore, while adolescent me may have been initially upset that the grown-up version bought that stock, the grown-up can take actions that the adolescent could not dream of taking.

Back on topic, we can start to address some of the things that we can do to tackle the problem of climate change. While there are concerted efforts to pass the responsibility for action solely upon us and not those causing the pollution, there are lots of things that we can do to help. Some of those things are getting solar, wind, or geothermal energy for our homes or businesses. Not only is this good for the Earth, but it will also save your bottom line.

We can also watch what we consume. For example, if we can cut out meat from one meal a week, that would help. Or at least switch to chicken for two meals. In addition, there are now better options to purchase a more fuel-efficient or electric vehicle when the current one needs to be replaced. Even if they run off coal power, electric vehicles account for 75% less emissions than internal combustion vehicles over their lifetime. At the very least, we can all recycle, and hopefully plant a tree.

But like I said earlier, if you are not able to do those things, there are still actions you can take. Such as writing to your representatives. Tell them to take this seriously. They respond to feedback (and money) because feedback means interest. It means we have a stake in helping to take care of this. This means continually engaging with them, regardless of party, will help them overcome their inertia. We can also encourage them to continue to invest in subsidies that make taking the above actions easier or remove the subsidies for fossil fuels.

In addition to the efforts we can make as individuals, there are things that we can do as a society to fix the issue. The first thing is investing in green energy technologies. We currently subsidize oil and gas far more than we subsidize green technologies. Just bringing them up to par would help fix this gap. Eliminating the subsidies that oil and gas receive would help push us financially away from those companies. Additionally, with the deregulation of the energy markets in the 1990s, nuclear power became cost prohibitive due to its high start-up costs and investment. Assisting them in overcoming this hurdle will help us meet our energy demands.

Green technologies are creating jobs across the country. As discussed earlier, increasing the amount of nuclear energy would be one thing. Another thing that can help that may not be terribly popular is carbon capture technologies. A fair complaint about them is that they may delay taking the big steps that will ultimately solve the problem, and while that is a fair complaint, we need to hit this problem hard. We need to be throwing as much as we can at this. Like I said before, if we wait for a perfect solution, we will be waiting forever.

Another way is by influencing the companies directly, such as purchasing stock and voting or voting with our wallets. As I will point out several times throughout this book, I am okay with rich people staying rich. Therefore, I am okay with the people currently in the power and energy fields staying in those fields. With that in mind, money is the best way to influence a company. We have a lot of power we are unaware of, specifically the power of our purse. We can spend our money with companies that do work to take care of the environment. Additionally, as a shareholder in an energy company, we can work to ensure that they research alternative forms.

One other thing to discuss before leaving this section, I mentioned it before, but I want us to take it to heart. We have to live in this society, and we must work and function here. So, if you are unable to make some of the changes here, there is no reason to feel shame. People tend to forget this, and certain media outlets love to use this talking point to sour the discussion. We are working to change society to make an environment where we can live. Until we get there, we must still live in this society. Therefore, when media personalities try and get people like Bernie Sanders with "gotcha" questions about why he uses planes to travel. He still needs to function in this society. The reason behind questions like that is to invalidate people that are trying to improve and repair our environment. Remember, 100 companies are responsible for 71% of the pollution. We're asking them to clean up a mess that they continue to make worse. If we get them cleaned up, then our society will have changed to be cleaner.

Chapter Twenty-Two

Stitching Us Together

In the first part of this book, we talked about who benefits from dividing us. Then, we talked about how the media and politicians used our fear and anger to gain power and influence. In this section, we talked about a lot of the issues that they use to remain in power and separate us. This led to us discussing ways to start taking back our power and working together to solve our problems.

Many of the problems discussed in this section had reasonable and relatively easy solutions that most of us agree upon. This means that we can work together to find common solutions. Sometimes it is hard to see another point of view, but that doesn't mean we shouldn't try.

Unfortunately, some groups still seek to exploit our divisions and make us fear each other. They use this division to further their own power and influence. While these groups tend to be in a minority of thought, they overwhelmingly influence policy.

For instance, in this section, we talked about gun rights and how a very small group keeps us from passing any laws that will save our children, under the belief that the first four words of the second amendment don't exist. In the next section, we will be talking about how a very small percentage of the population keeps fighting to remove the personhood or autonomy from others they don't like.

These groups have been successful at reframing arguments and discussions. They have successfully turned us against one another, furthering their political and financial power. They have even been successful at instituting their policies, despite their unpopularity. What I want you to take away from this is that if a small group of people can work for 40 years to redefine the second amendment, or coal and gas industries can lie to us for 70 years about the effects of climate change, then we can work together to fix our system.

We can no longer allow policies in this country to be set by people that want to manipulate and exploit us for their own power. Instead, we need to work together to fix our society. Whether that be by holding each other accountable for our actions or helping lift each other up to get the pay and benefits, we have worked for. We can fix our educational or justice systems. We can vote with our wallets and at the ballot box.

We can engage with one another and actually listen to one another. We have different experiences, and we can learn from people who are different from us. Be honest with one another. Civility is good, but if we aren't honest with one another, then we are only hurting ourselves. Being a melting pot is a good thing. It unifies us, even if we are different.

We can engage with our social and political action groups. We can empower the ones that are trying to make a positive change. They need our voices to be heard.

We can engage with our elected officials and remind them they work for us. We can encourage them that they need to work to repair the problems that they created. If we're obnoxious, they can't ignore us. If we're engaged, they know that you have a voice.

Chapter Twenty-Three

Major Hurdles

If you have made it this far in the book, then congratulations. However, this section will address some of the major points of contention we have in society. Because of this, I will be addressing specific concerns on each topic, but a lot of work needs to be done.

The topics addressed in this section are here because we no longer see each other as humans regarding any of these issues. I want that to stop. This section deals with issues in which people are dying. Or where people's existence is being outlawed.

I'll be honest, and in one of the earlier drafts of this book, this was a "kinder, gentler" section. However, my editors rightfully corrected me again because people are dying over these topics, which needs to stop. So, unlike the previous sections, there won't be as much talk about the validity of both sides of an argument.

Let me reiterate that this entire section is going to be talking about topics in which people are dying, or their existence is being outlawed. That's why there isn't a happy medium in this part. If there is one side asking to be recognized as authentic human beings and another wanting to erase them, there is no middle ground.

We need to break the cycle of demonizing and outlawing one another in order to preserve the ideals of our country. Many of these issues have come to a head in the past few years, and we have a lot of work to do to finish dealing with them so that we can move forward together. This section will make many people feel fairly uncomfortable, which is okay. Growth happens when you step outside your comfort zone.

This section will talk about some of the hard parts of our country and things that we do not like to discuss. One of the first things we will discuss is our history. Because it is one that is filled with heroes and monsters, we are being told that we need to view many of the monsters as heroes and forget about any of our actual heroes.

Additionally, we are going to talk about some of the divisions within our country, such as racism and homophobia, which manifest differently on both the left and the right. An example of how racism manifests is something that I learned about as a kid. In the south, people did not care if a black person got too close, but they cared about how high they got. In the north, people did not care about how high a black person got, but they cared about how close they were. For those not accustomed to the language, close means just that: they can be welcomed into your house and be your neighbors, but they cannot hold positions of authority. This was a simplistic and incomplete way of looking at it, but it does show how racism can manifest differently.

Additionally, we will be talking about the Lesbian, Gay, Bisexual, Transgender, and Queer (LGBTQ+) community. While there has been much forward progress in my lifetime on the matter, many people still would like to take us backward. For example, some states are actively trying to outlaw members of this community. Plus, some on the left feel like taking care of this community will actively harm their rights. So instead of working with them, they actively work against them.

Then I'm going to talk about abortion because who doesn't want to hear what a straight man has to say on the topic. For those curious, several dear friends of mine that have had abortions and were beta readers for this book encouraged me to be more direct in my language, so I will follow their guidance.

Moving on, I am going to talk about some of the institutional issues that we have in our country. There seems to be a lot of confusion going around about what is meant by institutional problems, and we will cover that throughout. This is also one of the reasons we have to start with a brief history lesson. Because if you don't know how an institution caused harm, then you can't see why it needs to be fixed.

Lastly, we are going to talk about the quintessential scare word in U.S. political discourse, socialism. We're going to talk about how it's used, and we are going to talk about the current capitalistic structure here in the U.S. Then, we will compare how those two relate to one another. A lot will be brought back up in this section, especially about employment and what we should all expect. Additionally, we will touch again on the power that we all have and how we can prevent others from exploiting us and using it for our collective good.

We can fix these issues. None of them is insurmountable. But we need to stop seeing people different from us as an "other." They are Americans. They are human. They need to be treated as such.

Chapter Twenty-Four

Accepting Our Entire History, Not Just the Myths

A major point of the past few years is that we must rethink how the history of the United States is being taught, specifically with regard to the civil war, our treatment of non-white people, and our treatment of workers. We have all grown up with myths surrounding our history, and unlearning those myths can be difficult. But learning the truth can better help us understand where we are and prepare us for the future.

There have been concerted efforts to hide parts of our history or not look at certain aspects. A better understanding of our history will help us identify the causes of our problems and will help us better fix those issues such as poverty or disparity. Plus, to paraphrase the analogy that Isabel Wilkerson has used to describe dealing with the issue of repairing the mistakes, we have made in our history: we have moved into a house that has problems, and while we may not be responsible for causing those problems, we are responsible for letting those problems get worse.

Recently there have been a lot of people that feel like history is being rewritten to something that they do not recognize. I would say that feeling is correct to those people, but that is because there is a lot about our history that we were never taught. Specifically, there have been intentional efforts to rewrite our history and culture to exclude the horrible reasons for the civil war and romanticize the south and the southern cause, or to make us forget about the use of company towns in the past. To not see how we have treated the poorest of our citizens.

By keeping us from learning about these events, it is harder for us to recognize their impacts on us today. For example, suppose we never learn about the damage caused by company towns. Then, when 'single enterprise communities' or 'innovation zones' are proposed, we don't see them for what they are, making it harder to stand up against them. Plus, if we don't learn how we have treated non-white populations, it is easier to blame them for their circumstances rather than see the problems that need to be fixed.

Suppose we never learn about how we spent decades destroying nonwhite communities after centuries of not letting them have a community. In that case, we question why they aren't on par with rich communities. If we never learn how we forced indigenous populations to land without resources, we don't question why they remain poor. If we never learn about how labor movements have been destroyed in this country, we can simply blame poor people for being poor and tell them that it's their fault.

Within the last few years, this has become a large topic of conversation because we are starting to come to terms with our past and making efforts to remove monuments to people that tried to overthrow our country. But unfortunately, some people believe that if statues of confederate generals come down, then we are erasing our history. They don't understand that these statues were erected to erase and change our history. We need to take that back and learn what has actually happened in our country, not a myth that causes far more harm.

Besides, every statue of a confederate general is someone that was a traitor to our country. If we want to celebrate the heroism of people during the Civil War, then there should be more monuments to people like Colonel Robert Shaw, who led a black regiment. When he was killed in combat, the confederates left his body in a mass grave with his black soldiers. They hoped this would disgrace and dishonor him, but his family stated that it was an honor for him to be buried with his men.

My education up to high school was deficient in a lot of ways. This isn't to disparage my teachers, but what they were allowed to teach was incomplete. For starters, how did we learn about the Civil War? In school, did we ever learn about the Tulsa massacre or the successful coup of a democratically elected government in Wilmington, NC? I grew up in North Carolina and had never heard about that. What about how Nazis came to the U.S. to learn about how to segregate people? How about the company towns that I mentioned earlier?

Some of us had to learn about them after becoming adults, but many of us are still unaware. Do you know what I'm talking about? If not, do not worry; I will provide a summary of these events. But I would highly recommend learning about each one of these topics in far greater detail than I'm going to provide.

There are fascinating and tragic aspects of our history. Ones that we can learn from so that we never repeat them. Unfortunately, we have not been taught these things; in many cases, history was rewritten to prevent us from learning them. Because they know that if we don't learn about them, then the same atrocities can be committed over and over again.

What did you learn about the Civil War? Was it called the War of Northern Aggression? I never heard it called the War of Northern Aggression in school, but I did hear it called that in the community. Were you taught that it was about states' rights? We still hear that argument today that it was about states' rights, but never which ones. It sort of was about states' rights, just not how we typically think. Northern states were not returning freed enslaved people to the south, and the southern states wanted the federal government to intervene. However, they did not because the northern states had the right not to return enslaved people.

Out of curiosity, lots of people think it was about states' rights and that the rebellion was to take off the yoke of an oppressive federal government. It isn't mentioned which rights it was fought over or the war specifically to keep an oppressive yoke on enslaved people. The articles of the confederation mention this point repeatedly and that enslaving black people was indeed the foundation of the confederation. It wasn't mentioned that the southern states had a problem because the federal government wasn't oppressing the northern states enough about returning their enslaved people.

The southern states wanted to continue enslaving people, but the northern states did not. The southern states specifically said they were seceding to ensure the "subordination to the superior race." It was absolutely about enslaving and subjugating people. Southern states made lots of money from owning people and using their forced labor to produce things. It makes sense that they did not want to give this up. It also makes sense that after losing the war, they created a lie to protect their "honor."

The education about the causes and division leading to the Civil War stops at states' rights and starts moving into military engagements. Then when the war was over, we were taught that our country no longer enslaved people, but was that true? How many of us learned about debt peonage, convict leasing, or simple debtors' prison, which kept a de facto state of enslavement going for long after the Civil War ended. It's not a coincidence that this type of coercive labor became used since slavery was outlawed for everyone except prisoners.

A movement after the Civil War promoted a "Lost Cause" mythology around the southern states and their reason for going to war. This "Lost Cause" myth is what shifted the conversation to one of "state's rights" against an oppressive federal government and did its best to eliminate the mention of enslaving people as a reason for the war. Additionally, this "Lost Cause" mythos is the one that introduced arguments like enslavement was good for black people, which is still heard today. Many people don't like to hear about the horrors of enslaving people, and some attempt to downplay it, but ignoring these horrors minimizes the problems they have caused today.

Most people will argue that Germany did some pretty horrific things in World War II. But what did Germany do postwar to confront its own past? First, they changed how they taught about that period of history. Instead of glamorizing their war efforts, they taught about how the Nazis came to power. They taught about the horrific things that occurred. Not to induce shame but to prevent those things from happening again. We can do the same thing with the Civil War, learn from the mistakes that led up to it and from the propaganda that mythologized people that enslaved others. We can also extend this lesson to all of our histories.

This conversation about the Civil War has been coming up a lot recently because there has been a lot of discussion about removing the statues commemorating southern leaders. Quick question, what if we made statues of Edward Snowden throughout the country? Or what if we made statues of Osama Bin Laden? What would the reaction be if someone thought we should do that to remember our history? Lots of people, myself included, would be furious. I am also willing to bet that some are upset at the comparison. However, what should we call people who willingly took up arms against the U.S. government? People like to oversimplify by making the Civil War about Gray vs. Blue, but recall that the "Blue" was the U.S. Army.

This leads us back to the "Lost Cause" and the rhetoric which has been played frequently in the media. Pundits and politicians love to go on television and say things like enslaved people were fortunate to be enslaved, to the point that people believe this lie today. Of course, because it is much easier to reframe horrific choices and actions than it is to be accountable for them, this lie continues to permeate our discourse. It was a very easy lie for the people that supported the cause of enslaving people to accept. Reinforcing this lie was in the best interests of the families of those fighting to keep a horrific system to convince people that the system was not horrible. But this lie prevents us from fixing the problems that remain because of this enslavement, much less the problems that have continued afterwards.

It should be noted that this lie is used every time that black people have fought for equality in this country. For example, most of the statues of confederate generals were put up during the civil rights movement. So why did all of these statues of people who fought to ensure black people would be permanently viewed as the property have a surge in popularity when those people wanted to be treated equally? Here is a hint, racism, specifically the people erecting those monuments, wanted to tell the people asking for equality that they were not equal.

If we truly want to remember heroes of this time and celebrate them in public, we could put up statues of people like Col Shaw or famous abolitionists like Harriet Tubman, William Garrison, Frederick Douglass, Angelina Grimké, John Brown, Harriet Beecher Stowe. But, if we really want to celebrate people who stood up for what was just from this era, we should learn more about these people. If we want to remember the people that stood for the best of our country's ideals, we should put up more of their statues.

Next, I wanted to discuss the Tulsa Race Massacre of 1921. This was when, what was known as, Black Wall Street was destroyed. In Tulsa, Oklahoma, there was a region known as Black Wall Street because of how wealthy the black residents were. For a very brief and oversimplified view, there was an accusation against a black man who was arrested. A white mob showed up to lynch him, and a black mob showed up to stop them. Violence ensued, leading many white people to storm Black Wall Street, destroying businesses, and killing people. It went so far that aircraft were used to bomb parts of the city. This was nearly erased in history and wasn't even discussed in Tulsa for a very long time. I first learned about the Tulsa Race Massacre watching the HBO show *Watchmen*. I was watching the opening scene, which depicted the destruction described above. I was shocked. I thought they had made something up for the show, but I also knew that the *Watchmen* had a habit of using real history to make a larger point. So, I looked it up and was amazed that not only was it a real thing that happened, but that it was much worse than what was depicted on screen.

If you are unfamiliar with these events, I recommend looking into them and learning more about them. Especially considering some of the lies we mentioned that came from the Lost Cause, specifically that black people liked being enslaved and that being an enslaved person was beneficial for them.

Plus, this early success amongst the black community shows that if they are allowed to succeed, they will.

Now back to an incident that is eerily familiar to something that happened recently. There was a coup against a fairly elected government by a group of white supremacists. Now to play the game, am I talking about January 6, 2021, or about November 10, 1898? The clue is that I said there was a coup, not an attempted coup. Many of us never learned about the coup to overthrow the government of Wilmington, NC, in 1898. Primarily because once it happened, there was an effort to erase it from history, not to hide the shame of the coup, but to prevent black people from knowing they could be fairly elected to office.

What happened? Basically, and very oversimplified, in the post-Civil War south, a group of white supremacists did not like the fact that blacks had been elected to local government, so they got together and killed them and destroyed their businesses. This was done, and people tried to erase it from history completely and were mostly successful.

It would be nice to think that this is only something that could happen far back in our history, but as I mentioned, this happened on January 6, 2021, at the U.S. capitol, when, again, white supremacists attempted to overthrow a fairly elected government. In fairness to the people throwing the 2021 coup, which is something I never thought I would type, they were lied to and manipulated into both believing there was something superior about being white and about the need to throw a coup, both of which will be covered in other sections of the book.

Later on, after the Civil War, we entered into what was known as a "Jim Crow" era of our history. Think "separate but equal." Plot twist, separate, but oh so not equal. How unequal? So unequal that Nazis came to the United States to learn about how to segregate their own populations. I feel like I do not need to mention how that went. But I will. They looked at our laws to keep blacks, immigrants, and Native Americans separate and used that information to create the ghettos later and eventually gas chambers. [1 2]

This is a perfect example of what happens when we don't learn about our history. We take great pride in standing up to the Nazis and defeating them in World War II. But we don't learn about how they based their crimes on what they learned from us. Now that we had twice failed in learning how Nazis were made when they came here to learn and how they took power in Germany, we are failing to recognize the growing neo-fascists in our own country again. Look at the protestors that came to Charlottesville and the movements that sprung up since then. We did not learn our own history; the worst parts of it are returning.

People know that if you lie about history, you can change how it is viewed. They know that they can influence future generations into believing the atrocities they committed were not really bad or that their ancestors, who I will remind you owned, beat, raped, and murdered people, were honorable because they occasionally fed the people they tortured. Then it is more likely that they or their descendants can commit these kinds of atrocities in the future.

Basically, it is very easy not to learn the mistakes of our history if we are never taught that history to begin with. But guess what, now we know (some of) those mistakes we have made, and we can do something. But unfortunately, we also know how we have been manipulated into not knowing these facts. Because if we do not know that our country is capable of these things, how can we stop them from happening again?

Now let's talk about company towns. These are towns that are generally built up around an industry, and historically, this applied to such industries as mining. Once this industry is established, then support businesses such as grocery stores and schools are built around it. This in and of itself isn't necessarily a bad thing. But the problem comes when the democratic process is undercut by allowing the business total control of the local government, most of which had no local government at all, with the company making all the decisions for the local population.

These were negative because they removed people's ability to self-govern. These towns, including the homes where the workers lived, were completely owned by a company. They could not advocate for better wages or benefits without the loss of both their jobs and their homes. They had no rights except those granted by their employer.

Now, with this very brief overview of a couple of historical topics, let's move on to how this affects events happening in the present day. Would we do these things now? Even our recent history has seen efforts to undermine our efforts to work together and prevent exploitation. We have seen a resurgence of company towns, now rebranded as "Innovation Zones." We never knew the lessons of our history, so we continue to repeat the mistakes we made.

One example of more recent history that has affected our current situation is the story of Robert Moses. He is someone that chose to destroy black and Puerto Rican communities to build roads and expand the suburbs for white communities in New York City. Unfortunately, his actions enabled others to do similar actions in other cities throughout the country, further entrenching the wealth inequality throughout our country.

Notice that we keep doing that to non-white people. They start to get a little bit, and we literally destroy what they have. Then we see people in our media blame them for not having good homes and schools, which are dependent upon property values.

We get to blame them for being poor and living in high-crime areas. Then we get to tell them they need to pull themselves up by their bootstraps, which originated as a saying to mean something which is impossible. These problems still exist in liberal and conservative areas, with people on the left advocating for social programs to help the disadvantaged while hypocritically ensuring that those programs, such as affordable housing, are nowhere near them. Ignoring what past actions caused our present problems does not allow us to fix them.

Another example has been an expansion to the keystone pipeline being built, which is redundant. A pipeline already transports oil along the route, and the expansion is for a shortcut. So, any discussion about the need for a pipeline is thrown out the window since it already exists. I know a lot of people probably were unaware of that fact because it is withheld from us. Additionally, it wouldn't create permanent jobs, increases the amount of pollution in our environment, and doesn't even supply the U.S. with oil. But how does this pertain to our current topic?

Well, because people's homes and land are being destroyed and poisoned by oil leaks, to make this shortcut? Does it matter that the homes and land being destroyed belong to indigenous people? But why was the indigenous people's land being used in the first place? Because the original route cut through a town of people who voted that it shouldn't go through their neighborhoods. The controversy only started because of the decision to take it through indigenous people's lands. Which also violated several treaties. No one complained when the town didn't want it going along the original path.

Now, before anyone gets on a political high horse, politicians of both parties have supported the pipeline and have changed their minds under enormous political pressure. This is just one example, but it shows that we are still willing to destroy the homes and land of people just for a little convenience.

We have a history of tearing down minority neighborhoods and destroying their accomplishments in the name of progress. We still do this while dealing with the repercussions of past actions, which persist to this day. We have to acknowledge them in order to move forwards. Shining a light on the dark parts of our history is the first step in amending and atoning those actions.

What do I want us to take away from this section? I do not want to rewrite or forget our history. I want us to learn it. I want us to go out and actually learn our history, not just the flowery parts that make us feel comfortable. If we learn about the tragic things that we have done, we are more likely to prevent those atrocities from occurring in the future.

I do not want us to take away shame or guilt. I want us to take away an understanding that the history we have been taught is incomplete. I recommend we look into the historical subjects I brought up more.

I strongly recommend learning the bad stuff about our history as well. The good stuff is awesome and nice to know. But if we do not learn where we faltered, we will make those mistakes again in the future. Plus, there are a lot of cases where we have learned from our mistakes; growth is always a positive sign. It is never too late to learn and grow, and as my cousin (in-law) pointed out when she was 10, you have to challenge yourself to grow. She will always be one of my favorite people for this statement alone.

We also must stop the concerted effort taking place right now to prevent us from learning about our history. Many states have passed laws to prevent our children from learning anything that might make them "uncomfortable," or "guilty," or stray from this myth of the country. There are uncomfortable parts of our history. Learning it helps us come to terms with where we are now.

There are very positive aspects of our history that we haven't been taught, that we will discuss elsewhere in this book. Things like we used to have universal childcare or that tuition, was free at many colleges for a long time. Or times when companies used to invest in their workers and their communities. If we think that the working and educational conditions are the way they've always been in this country, then there is not enough inertia to overcome these problems. But if we know that we used to have these programs and that they helped us to become hugely successful, then we can push to have that reform.

---

1. Ross, Alex. "How American Racism Influenced Hitler", The New Yorker, April 23, 2018, https://www.newyorker.com/magazine/2018/04/30/how-american-racism-influenced-hitler.
2. Katznelson, Ira. "What America Taught the Nazis", The Atlantic, November 2017, https://www.theatlantic.com/magazine/archive/2017/11/what-america-taught-the-nazis/540630/.

Chapter Twenty-Five

All Lives Should Matter, But Right Now They Don't

Think about this, in 2020; a video came out of people hunting down a man. They chased him down in a truck while he was jogging. They hunted him because they thought he did not belong. He was jogging. There is video proof of him being hunted and murdered by these people. Yet if there was no video, the people who hunted him would have gotten away with it.

The video of the event was even released by one of the assailants to show why they needed to hunt this man down. Which worked in their favor for a while as multiple prosecutors refused even to charge these men with a crime. Only after a large amount of political backlash were these men eventually charged and convicted of their crimes.

Unfortunately, this is just one of several examples of black people being murdered alone at the beginning of 2020. Several of the more notable ones were murdered by police officers.

Many people were upset by Colin Kaepernick taking a knee to protest murders like these, but how upset were they by these murders? There are far too many people that are more upset by the protests than the murders. What does that say about you and your view of justice if you are one of them?

Colin Kaepernick and many others were protesting by taking a knee during the national anthem played before sporting events. They took action after a military member told him how to protest in a respectful way to the anthem. He was protesting the sanctioned murder of black people by the state. So sanctioned because these murders often went without punishment or consequence, becoming a de facto sanction.

Instead of listening to what these protests were about, they were distorted by right-leaning media and politicians to mean that these protestors did not support the troops. Of course, this was blatantly false, but it served as a narrative. That being that they did not want to address systemic problems we have, specifically the disproportionate killing of black people by members of the police, and would rather change the topic and not address any of the issues.

Manipulating the discourse around black lives is not limited to conservative politicians and media. On the flip side, to the white liberals, is "Black Lives Matter" just a slogan? Is it just a platform to get Democrats elected? Once Biden was elected, what happened to that cause? What happened to the anger about injustices, or was there more support for things returning to "normal"? Remember that "normal" includes the killing that was being protested.

If you are angry about such questions, think about how upset some leaders in the black community are with using black lives as a political platform rather than a movement to bring their lives to parity with white lives. What happened to the time and money being given to work on this issue since the election?

Let me hit a few key points as a primer for those that may have misconceptions about this topic. Many of us have been told that the "Black Lives Matter" movement is a domestic terrorist threat? If so, this is a lie.

I know we have been told this through our media and social media. We are constantly lied to about this. Because if they can convince us that black people are the reason for hardships in our life or that they are coming for our stuff or hurting our family, then we will fight them. To be fair, this is a tactic that has been employed against numerous groups of people throughout our history, and it is a reliable fear tactic. We get afraid, and they get to manipulate us.

A very sizable chunk of the media within the U.S. went out of their way to disparage the largest civil rights movement in the country. They want things to stay the same, which hurts poor and minority communities. This is why wanting things to return to "normal" doesn't help to improve lives.

Instead, the truth is that many things that the "Black Lives Matter" movement is asking for will improve the lives of non-black people too. Reforming the police, improving education, and ensuring that this country provides equal opportunity are some of the things being requested. But unfortunately, there are many people scared that providing equal opportunity means taking away from them, so they make sure we do not work together or find common ground.

What is the "Black Lives Matter" movement trying to accomplish then? There are several ways to think about this, but I like the firefighter example. Think about it this way; there is a fire at a neighbor's house. Therefore, they need to have the firefighters at their house right now. Stopping the firetrucks and saying all houses matter is not going to help. Letting the people who need it get the help they need. Right now, we have come to see that there is a fire at the house of our black neighbors.

What help do black people need? I think it is reasonable for the state to provide them with the same opportunities as white people. They aren't asking for white people to have less privileges; they are asking for the same. They want to be able to work hard, build businesses, and create opportunities for their children. They want to be able to do this without fear of being shot or their businesses burned down simply for being black.

Frankly, I do not see the problem with this. They are asking for accountability with police when they are more violent with them than non-black people. Oddly enough, one of the responses I have seen from conservatives about this is that there are bad cops that hurt members of every community. To which I question, why don't we fix that? If we recognize the problem, we have allies who want to fix it. The Black Lives movement wants to fix it.

Think about it this way; the black community does not want to be murdered by the state in the same way that the state did not murder the January 6th insurrectionists. In fact, the insurrectionists murdered one police officer and hurt numerous others. Meanwhile, they were not met with tear gas, rubber bullets, and the National Guard. Unlike the Black Lives Matter protests, which did receive that level of treatment.

Many people want us to believe that there is no longer racism in this country. Both liberal and conservative media outlets like to rely upon the fact that we elected a black man as president to state that we are no longer racist. However, even if that were true on an individual level, there are so many policies we had in place for so long that have harmed black communities that we need to take action to fix them.

What policies am I talking about? Only a few decades ago did we stop the practice of redlining, which prevented blacks from owning property. The civil rights acts were passed, preventing them from being discriminated against in voting practices, and schools were integrated. But this didn't stop the destruction of communities for overpasses or pipelines, both of which actively avoided white neighborhoods.

As we discussed, poor and minority schools are perpetually underfunded. Minority homeowners have their homes undervalued. Minority-owned businesses are less likely to get a business loan, and if they do, it has a lower balance and higher interest rate. Qualified minorities are not promoted to executive positions. There are still plenty of problems that need to be fixed.

This section has mainly focused on the inequalities being faced by the black community. The treatment they have received has been at the forefront of the news recently; however, these issues are not theirs alone.

There has been a drastic increase in violence against the Asian community, who were blamed for the pandemic. As such, they have had to face a sharp increase in violence. They have also been treated like a sexual fetish. Then when they get murdered by someone who fetishized them, a police captain says that the murderer was just having a bad day.

Before this, Asians had repeatedly been called a "model minority." This itself is due to only allowing highly skilled professionals to immigrate to the U.S. This "model minority" status was developed and is still used to drive a wedge between them and other minorities.

Latinos also face a great deal of discrimination in our country. They have been accused of coming to steal our jobs while being very lazy. Racism doesn't make sense. Popular politicians and presidents have described them as drug dealing rapists. Generally, they are accused of these things by the same party that espouses family and religious values. Things have historically been a large part of Latino communities. The separation caused by racism prevents the strength that unity brings.

What should we do to fix this problem? Well, the first thing is fairly simple, recognize the basic humanity in other people.

Talk to people and learn about their different experiences. No group is a monolith. When you see someone engaging in behavior that dehumanizes another group of people, call them out on it. That's how we can start to address it on an individual level.

Also, do not assume that someone that disagrees with you is racist. To my liberal friends, there are plenty of non-white people that are conservative. Being conservative does not mean that you are automatically a racist. Find people that are different from you and get to know them as a person. This closeness helps. Neither of you must give up your basic humanity or your own culture. Love does cancel hate, and many of us believe that too.

Something that I have seen expressed from conservatives towards liberals and that I think bears repeating. Do not use black people as symbols or puppets for political gain. Here is the thing, I know that as many white liberals will be upset by this, many non-white liberals will see this as a reality. To paraphrase a sentiment, I have heard from the black community that addresses the same concern, how many have conducted performative acts of anti-racism, such as the black square on Instagram feeds, but haven't done any work. On a bright note, here is something that different sections of our population agree upon.

What do I want us to do? Get to know our neighbors as human beings and treat them as such. Non-white people are not asking for white people to be treated as poorly as they are; they are asking to be treated as well as white people. Once that happens, all lives will truly matter, not just be a slogan used when black people ask not to be murdered.

Chapter Twenty-Six

No One is Replacing You

We are going to talk about a few different concepts in this section. But the main takeaway is that if a group achieves equality, that does not take away from the groups in power. To put this more bluntly, if brown and black people have the same opportunities as white people, that does not mean they are now oppressing white people.

When Nazis and white supremacists descended upon Charlottesville, Virginia, they were protesting the possible removal of monuments to traitors to the country. While marching, they indicated that they were worried about being replaced, whether by non-white people or by Jews. This "replacement theory" has taken hold in the minds of many people and has been promoted as a legitimate concern in the media.

Some groups of white people are convinced that we should not acknowledge how our society benefits them. They are being told that white people are being marginalized and discriminated against. They are being told that they are a monolith.

They are being told that everyone who isn't white is trying to destroy them. Nothing is further from the truth.

What does it mean to be white? This may be hard to believe, but the definition has changed over the centuries. It changed because it was originally designed to exclude people, not include them, and it continues to serve that purpose.

Did you know that Irish people used not to be considered white? Did you know that Italians were not considered white either? That is because the entire concept of being white is made up. It is an illusion meant to suppress people, specifically nonwhite people. That is why the definition keeps changing.

There is no inherent significance to skin color. But the significance was invented as a way to ensure that people of European ancestry saw themselves as a collective. A collective that could then declare itself superior. It is this culture of superiority that is toxic to all of us.

This culture has enabled a barrier to obstruct access to resources for many non-white people. It is the lack of these obstacles that constitute "white privilege."

Let me illustrate what "white privilege" is with a personal anecdote and why removing it is in the best interest of everyone, white people included.

My early life was not one of privilege. I grew up poor, very poor, and I was homeless for a little while too. I have an alcoholic father who was absent for most of my life and does not remember abusing me. My mom had to work several jobs while going to school to ensure that my sister and I had better opportunities.

Fortunately, my mother instilled within me a high value for education. Because of this, all people could see was that I was a white boy who could speak well. Therefore, my background did not matter as much to those around me.

I was never denied access wherever I went, and people still thought that I would end up in the big house on the hill. I felt like people did not see me for who I was. This left me angry. I hated the assumptions people made about me, and I did not understand why they felt that way. It is this anger that I let go of, and if you are feeling it, it is this anger that I want you to let go of. It is like the Buddhist quote: "Holding onto anger is like drinking poison and expecting the other person to die."

Here is what I'm saying. My white skin did not serve as a barrier for me at all. In fact, it did open doors. My non-white friends, who worked just as hard as I did, also had to live in a society that devalued them because of their skin color. Those doors that automatically opened for me didn't open for them.

I never had to deal with people calling me racial slurs or security following me through a store. I never had to worry about being attacked because of my skin color. I never worried about the police.

I tell you this because while I was a beneficiary of white privilege, I did not know it at the time, and I had, and have, no control of that privilege. If you're white, the same holds for you. Your life may not have been easy, but your skin color did not hold you back. You may not have been aware of the privilege, and you did not have a role in creating that system and probably have no control over that system.

But we need to provide this privilege to everyone because white privilege can be deadly. To illustrate this, how about a side-by-side comparison. Dylan Roof murdered nine people at a church in Charleston, and not only was he arrested without incident, but the officers also provided him with Burger King before taking him to prison.

Conversely, there is the case of Jemel Roberson, a security guard that had subdued a gunman. However, when police arrived on the scene, they quickly shot and killed him. He was a uniformed security guard who had stopped a person actively trying to murder people. He was protecting his community yet was treated like a threat.

This is one of many examples where white people who betray their community are still cared for, while black people who protect their communities are still treated as a threat. Now, just to remind you, black people do not want white people to be treated as a threat; they just want to be treated humanely. They want the same privilege. However, that does not remove the one in place.

I know at this point, people are probably feeling guilty for being white. This is not a productive way to handle the situation. This guilt can manifest in several ways, from things like self-deprecation or wallowing to things like fetishization or infantilization. None of this helps the problems that we have been talking about. In the same way, you would not ask a black person to feel guilt for being born black, and you do not need to feel guilt for being born white.

Now onto my asks for this section. To white people, acknowledge that white privilege is real. Your life may not have been easy, but your skin color was not a barrier. Next, use that privilege to help people. Call it out when you see someone not receiving equal treatment, merely because of their skin color.

The damage done to non-white communities is real and needs to be fixed. Whether you believe we should be a meritocracy or that we all need to care for each other, these privileges need to be shared. That will remove needless obstacles for people to succeed.

Next is not to use this debate over privilege as a hammer to beat other people. Instead, you can get them to work with you and progress towards a common goal without them searching their souls.

Lastly, whether or not you have, or recognize that you have, privilege, work together to solve our problems. Most of us dream that this country can be the land of equal opportunity. If you have that privilege, use it to help others remove the barriers in their lives.

Now let's move on to talk about white supremacy, and there will be a few points that will be hard to read. But I do not want that to dishearten you. We can all see the harm being done to our country by white supremacists.

Just as I wrote about white guilt being counterproductive, feelings of pride in being born white are also misplaced. These feelings of having, or needing to prove, supremacy over others have led to horrific acts of terror and violence here in the United States.

Before we go down this path, I want to clarify a few things. First, while I am talking about far-right extremists in this section, that does not mean all people on the right are either extremists or believe in white supremacy. Second, while extremists on the left have killed people, the extremists on the right have killed nearly 20 times as many Americans.

Let me reiterate those points, but first to the liberal readers. There are a very large number of conservatives that are not white or are married to people that are not white. It is massively disingenuous to call all conservatives racists or to lump them in with extremists. In fact, I know a lot of non-white conservatives who have only felt racism at the hands of white liberals. Many conservatives find white supremacists reprehensible but want to be treated as an individual. We can work together to solve this issue.

To my conservative readers, white supremacists use your language to recruit members. They speak of freedom and opportunities to lure in members. They speak of overcoming hardships to improve their lives. But their message takes yours, twists it, and directs it towards disillusioned, or disaffected, white people. That's how you get media outlets talking about 'replacement theory,' That's how you get white-collar Nazis marching in Charlottesville.

These people are wearing clothing or waving flags declaring their white supremacist ideology and showing up at your rallies. Even though you are not on their side, they are on your side and think you agree with them. Therefore, they need to be shown to stand apart from your ideals.

These people showing up to your rallies should not be ignored, as they tend to be some of the loudest people in terms of volume and actions. They tend to take the conversation away from whatever the subject may be to theirs. Also, it is not enough to simply not like these people; you must actively stand up to these extremists. Their ideas must be challenged when they are presented.

The second point concerning the level of violence speaks to what I have just talked about. The level of violence committed by these people, who falsely proclaim themselves to be conservative, is one of the greatest threats to our country. They are actively killing Americans, like Heather Heyer.

A couple of examples of how the lies of white supremacy have infiltrated conservative thought can be found in protests that have occurred recently. However, these protests have also shown a stark contrast between how people are treated while protesting based on their skin color.

During the summer of 2020, there were many protests regarding the murder of black people by state agents and the Black Lives Matter movement. They were told that they were protesting wrong and that their points should be disregarded since some people were being violent. Note that the point of the protests was that agents of the state should not murder people.

Other forms of protest were tried, such as taking a knee during the anthem of sporting events, but they were told that was wrong too. By the way, they took a knee because a Green Beret told Kaepernick that was a respectful way to protest. However, even this form of bringing attention to the problem was disrespectful and traitorous.

Two of the responses to the Black Lives Matter movement were the Blue Lives Matter and the All Lives Matter lines of discourse. First, both of those lines of argument disregarded the requests from Black Lives Matter without ever listening to them. There were lies almost immediately about what the Black Lives Matter movement stood for and what they were protesting to achieve.

Almost all media coverage focused on the negative aspects of these protests and enjoyed showing burning buildings. Which speaks to the lies we're told by the media we discussed previously. As a result of these lies, many people are very upset at the mere mention of Black Lives Matter. That shows that these lies are very effective and why some media outlets even refer to them as terrorist groups. Especially since all these people wanted was not to be killed by the state.

Comparatively, on January 6th, 2021, a group of insurrectionists stormed the U.S. Capitol building in DC, hoping to scare the legislation into overthrowing the presidential election of 2020. This action was taken by people who were lied to by numerous politicians and media outlets about their power being stolen. They were told this to ensure power for politicians and media outlets and to cement the lies they were spreading. These people were even told to descend upon the capitol to prevent a lawful election from taking place.

The police response to the insurrection was very different from those of the Black Lives Matter protests. There was a minimal police presence at the start. However, during the insurrection, a police officer was drug out of the capital and beaten with an American flag while those beating him shouted "USA, USA." The same politicians that lied to instigate the insurrection lied again to say that there was no attack on the capital; instead, it was just a bunch of angry people.

The fact that right-wing extremists are causing so much violence is something that has not been getting enough honest attention in the media. It is either downplayed, ignored, fallen victim to "both sides" -ism, or politicians are just lying about what is happening. For example, most of us probably did not know that far-right extremists killed nearly 20 times as many people as far-left extremists, but they are portrayed in similar lights. Or you have politicians that instigate violence, like the January 6th insurrection, but then blame it on Antifa, who was not there. This makes it hard to talk about or do anything if we are constantly being lied to or misled about reality.

These far-right extremists are gaining enough political clout that states like Oklahoma and Florida have passed legislation allowing people to run over and kill protestors without repercussion. People who are exercising their first amendment rights are now allowed to be murdered in those states lawfully. What would you think if someone passed legislation that you were allowed to be murdered for protecting your second amendment rights? Work together to end this.

Now on to the people that have been, or are currently being, tempted by the falsehood of white supremacy. I know many of you think you are being discriminated against for being white, but you are not. Your life may not be easy, and you may have experienced unfairness, but you cannot take out your anger and frustration on other groups of people because it is not their fault. No one is trying to replace you or eliminate you.

The lie of white supremacy can be very seductive. They say things that are true, like you may be in pain or that you may be going through problems that are not your fault. But then they offer the lie that it is the fault of groups of people based on their skin color or heritage.

It might be that your wages have been stagnant, and there is little hope for promotion, or you lost your job. It may be a personal problem in your life. This is when they come in with false empathy for your plight and then lie to you about the cause, such as Mexicans taking your jobs or that Jews are trying to replace you. These lies need to be challenged and rejected. As former white supremacists have said, their arguments fall apart the moment a white person challenges their lies.

Liberals can say stupid things, as I address throughout this book, but they are not advocating for another holocaust; they are not advocating to erase all the horrible things that have happened in this country in the name of white supremacy. Want to talk about the damage this country has done to non-white people and poor people, and doing it in a simplistic, sometimes offensive manner is not the same as literal murder. These things are not equal.

Here's the thing, yes, the pain and helplessness that these people feel are real. The desire to take action is real. However, here are a couple of painful truths. The people convincing you to join up with Nazis and terrorists do not want to actually heal your pain. They want to take your power and use it for their goals. The second is that the best way to deal with this pain is not to attack others. It is to work through the problem. Get help if you need to; we all need it from time to time.

The first point about them not wanting to heal your pain speaks to the origins of white supremacy. Those in power have always wanted to divide us and redirect the anger and pain that some of us feel away from fixing the problems and towards each other.

Think about it; you're worried about feeding your family or ensuring your children's future. You're worried about the future. Two of the options available to the people wishing to manipulate you are to either fix the issues that are causing these problems, which is harder, or to convince you that your problem is caused by other people.

The second point is that you should not use your pain to attack others. As you know, the best way to deal with a problem is to do the hard work. Directing your anger towards other groups of people is counterproductive and ultimately prevents you from focusing on the hard work needed to fix the issue.

The most important ask I can have in this section is to see the humanity in one another. It's the theme of the entire book.

Second, erase the idea of white supremacy, and heal those who hold those beliefs. Realize that it is a separate concept from regular conservative thought. They are not intertwined.

To the liberals, treat people as individuals. If they are in pain, help them. Do not think that all conservatives share the ideals of the far right.

For the conservatives, ensure your voices are separate from those that show up to your rallies promoting Nazism, the Confederacy, and white supremacy in general. I know many conservatives that personally condemn these beliefs, but an active role must be taken to help untangle these individuals.

Both need to realize that the media tends to play to the message they are trying to get across. Realize that when one side protests, you probably do not get the entire picture. Therefore, try to see it from the perspective of the protestors. The insurrectionists genuinely believed that the election was stolen. Would you do no less if you thought the same?

To those that believe that the whites are superior, realize that taking pride in your skin being white is harmful, both to yourself and others. It's not your heritage and is used to divide you from other people. Second, do not support people encouraging you to hate other people, and support the people willing to do the hard work to fix the issues that are affecting you. Black people and Mexicans are not taking your jobs; they are not coming here to rape women. We are being told this to distance ourselves from our fellow Americans.

Chapter Twenty-Seven

Members of the LGBTQIA+ are People Too

First, people are not born wrong, and the things that make us individually different can make us stronger as a community. Unfortunately, though this is something that still needs to be addressed, people have been, and still are, hated and discriminated against because of how they were born for far too long.

For those that still believe the lie that people choose to live this way and that we all fit into neat boxes, I have something to think about before we get started. Many of us are aware of hermaphrodites, now called Intersex, who took their name from a Greek god, Hermaphroditus. As a species, we have known for thousands of years that there are more than two sexes, i.e., we are not binary. Additionally, older generations have used terms like "girly man" or "man's man," as well as "tomboy" to differentiate between genders. Hence, they are already familiar with the concept of fluidity, even if they are unaware of that fact.

If you are a straight, cis-gendered person, do you remember how old you were when you realized you were a boy or a girl? How about when you realized you liked boys or girls? It may never have occurred to people who are straight and cis, who line up with what society expected. But there wasn't a choice there either.

I remember the first time a friend came out to me. In the late 1980s, people were still being murdered for being gay. I was scared for him, especially when he came out to our school. But, for him, it was a freeing experience. He realized who he was and decided to be honest about it, most importantly with himself but also everyone else. I imagine a lot of people have similar stories, either a loved one coming out or realizing that you did not fit what was defined as the norm.

Let's start with a few concepts. The first is about orientation, then sex, which will touch on genetics, followed by gender, and the last is about consent. These will help frame the topics we discuss, and a lot of the concepts that I bring up I have been taught by other people. So, if there is something that you don't understand, feel free to ask someone.

Frankly, there is a lot that I have had to learn over the years with some of these, so I expect that it can take some time to digest some of the things that I bring up. If this is your first time hearing these concepts, I would ask you to learn more about them and know the people that are within these communities.

The first thing is about orientation. This means what are you attracted to (men, women, both, neither, etc.). This takes up the LBG and A portions of the acronym above (Lesbian (women who like women), Bisexual (people who like men and women), Gay (men who like men), and Asexual (people that may be fine with a romantic relationship but aren't that interested in sex)). Of course, not everyone fits neatly into one of these categories, but they can serve as a decent starting point to understanding the basics.

Do you remember when you discovered what you were attracted to? You probably did not think about it; you were just attracted to some people and not others. What I am getting at it is that it was not a choice. You did not wake up one morning and decide that one type of person was more attractive than another; it just was.

Here's the thing, it's like that for everyone. If you did not get to choose, neither does anyone else. If they like the same gender as them, then that's how they were made. They did not get to choose that.

The second thing is about sex. These are the biological parts that you are born with. Most people are born with one set of clearly identifiable parts. However, many people are not. They are called Intersex and are the "I" in the acronym. While this is considered genetically rare, it is as common as redheads. This is also the community formerly known as hermaphrodites.

Historically people have tried to force people like that into one role or another, usually through genital mutilation, which may or may not line up with what their brain thinks is true. This causes lots of distress and pain to the child, especially as they grow. Please, note that I am not talking about trans people here, although the lesson still applies.

While talking about sex, let's hit on the topic of genetics because this and the parts between your legs are brought up in discussions all the time by people claiming that there are only two sexes. Ok, are you ready to learn something you may not have known? Your genetics do not have to match the parts between your legs. I didn't know it until relatively recently, either.

This means that your genetics can be coded for one sex, but you have the parts of the other one. Plus, without a genetic screening, you will never know. But that's okay because ultimately, it doesn't really matter. It is important to know because people are trying to legislate on that matter. On top of that are your hormones, which only makes things more confusing because they don't have to match either your parts or your genetics.

Next is gender. This is how we identify ourselves (male, female, nonbinary, etc.). This is where the Transgender part of the community (the "T" in the above) comes into play.

If you have never had someone in your life that is Trans, then this can be an unfamiliar topic. Therefore, I will paraphrase it the way a six-year-old described it. It's like having a boy's brain in a girl's body or vice versa. Side note, cis is a term from chemistry, where two things line up together. So, using this example, a cisgender male is a person with a male brain in a male body.

I don't use that example to disparage; I have known many Trans people throughout my life, and I still thought that was one of the best ways to explain it. Because it sometimes helps to have a kid explain something to me, I thought it would help.

This means that from very early on, they may feel like they are in a body that doesn't match who they are. This can lead to depression and anxiety, which is one reason suicide is so high among this group.

Just to clarify a couple of points I hear made in the media. Trans people do not want to go back and forth. They want their body to reflect who they are on the inside. It also does not mean men going to the women's restroom. It means men going to the men's and women going to the women's restroom. Trans people are not predators because they have to go pee.

In fact, if the concern is legitimately about preventing the wrong gender from going to the wrong bathroom, then trans people are absolutely on that side. They want to be allowed to go to the right bathroom and do not want people to harass them for doing so. They are an ally in this, but they just want you to accept them for their gender, which is different from the sex they were born with.

All this means that things like conversion therapy are torturous. It means that passing laws saying they cannot go to the bathroom is just wrong. It means forcing men to play women's sports or vice versa is wrong. People like to hold up examples of trans doing well in a sport to show that they should not be allowed to compete, but when trans athletes don't perform well, they are degraded. Just let them play.

This also further illustrates that saying like "hate the sin, love the sinner" have always been a false dichotomy. They do not get a choice; it's how they were made; it's not a sin. Just like the way you were made is not a sin. Statements like that are a way to continue hating someone for how they were born. You're not showing love.

The last thing to discuss is consent. However, there is a lot more that could be written about the subject than I will include here. Consent is a very important factor in any relationship. This is the permission to engage in certain activities each time they occur.

To borrow a concept, there is a video that illustrates this point using the concept of riding a bike. If you want to go bike riding with someone, you need their permission. They are also allowed to wear safety equipment.

You need their permission to go bike riding every time you go together. All because you went bike riding with someone does not mean that they may want to ride a bike with you in the future. If you want to go mountain biking and they don't, then you can't go together. Plus, you cannot ride a bike with someone if they are asleep or are inebriated through drugs or alcohol.

Does that all make sense? To have intercourse with someone, you both need to agree on what you're going to do each time you do it. Also, you should not force someone to do something that they are uncomfortable with.

I included consent in this discussion because people use pedophilia and bestiality as arguments against denying people their rights, such as marriage equality. People argue that we should not learn about these basic concepts such as gender, sex, identity, and consent because that is grooming. In fact, it is the opposite; learning these things about yourself can help you from being taken advantage of in relationships.

So let me clarify, kids cannot offer consent, and neither can animals. Grown adults consenting to a relationship is not the same. Stop trying to compare them. It's insulting.

Part of the reason I bring up consent is that some people like to use a slippery slope argument when talking about consent and rights for people that are not cis and straight. They like to ask where it ends as if that is a good argument for denying people their rights. It is very simple, it ends when people are accepted for who and what they are, and they are allowed to have a consensual relationship with the people they want.

But let us bring it back to the purpose of this section because I have not written about that in a while. The biggest one is to realize that orientation, sex, and gender are more complicated than we may realize. There are, and never were, neat little boxes for people to fit into. Yes, some people fit into neat little boxes, but that is not the limitation of human experience.

Another argument I hear against moving to a place in society where we recognize these people is that liberals think that these definitions are meaningless, and they think that people can be a boy or a girl depending upon the day or their mood. I hear you. I know you are being told that information. But it is not true. That is not what they want.

If all this information is new to you, or you have not had someone in your life that is homosexual or transgender, then you have not experienced it. You do not have that connection, so that it can be confusing. I get that. Like I said above, despite having people close to me that were part of the community, I have had people explain it to me like I am an idiot. To be fair, their experience is completely different from mine, so when it comes to their experience, I am an idiot, and I need to listen. The same goes for all of us when we are listening to an experience that is completely different from our own.

Although for everyone, here is something to remember. Respect each other. If someone asks you to use a different pronoun, then respect that. It costs you nothing but demonstrates your respect for the other person.

Finally, I have heard that people are using the fact that so many people are coming out as trans as evidence that liberals are destroying this country or making it weaker. Let me make a counterpoint, so many people are coming out as trans now because it is safer. They know that while they may not be completely accepted, they will not be systematically murdered, and there will be a safe place for them. We are seeing them more now because we have decided that it is no longer okay to harass, abuse, or outright murder them. Now we just must treat them like people (because they are).

This means the most important ask I have for you is going to be very simple as well. Treat people with love and compassion. If they come out to you, acknowledge it as a huge sign of trust. If they are trans, and you knew them before their transition, then go with them on this change. If you did not know them beforehand, then you have no excuse not to call them by what they are.

The next ask is to reject the lies these people coming forward somehow undermine or destroy our society. Having people acknowledge their true selves is a good thing. Having people consent to be in a loving, committed marriage is good. These make our society stronger.

The last ask is to reach out to your leaders and get them to overturn legislation that outlaws trans people. So many states have decided to outlaw people's rights to body autonomy or decide what bathroom they are allowed to use. They are even saying that trans girls can't play sports, which, if it were about fairness, they wouldn't allow trans boys either, but they don't seem to notice them. Don't legislate hate.

Chapter Twenty-Eight

Abortion and Women's Right to Their Body

This section is going to be different because instead of just focusing on the truth and lies surrounding this topic, I also want to focus on reminding people to be compassionate towards one another. Because right now, we are not compassionate when discussing this issue. We are very passionate, but that is not the same thing.

First, we are very passionate because this issue brings up strong feelings in all of us, and because of this, we tend to not listen to one another. Because of these feelings, we tend not to listen to one another regarding this topic.

But I want us to listen to each other more on this topic. I want us to recognize the humanity within each other as we discuss this difficult topic.

Let's start somewhere happy, and just a heads up, I'm going to make this a "Pollyanna" type story. A family decides to have a baby or decides not to use any form of protection, which is another way to make the same decision. They end up getting pregnant. Everyone, the couple, their friends, and family, and even strangers, is excited about the future possibilities for the new family. There is excitement about potential and change.

In this scenario, which is a fair number of people, this is all a happy event. The pregnancy and the future possibilities that it represents are celebrated.

The excitement is over possibilities. It's over, potentially bringing a new life into the world. Things could change. Miscarriages happen, and when they do, the couple mourns for lost possibilities and what might have been a child.

When someone has had a planned pregnancy, we celebrate with them. When someone has an unexpected miscarriage, we mourn with them. We should be there for one another during each of these times because even the joyous ones are stressful.

So now we move on to the decision to end those possibilities before they have begun. In so doing, I will ask again to talk to one another, even about issues that are as divisive as this. Treat each other with compassion.

If you don't know this already, you know at least one person that has had an abortion. Frankly, you probably know more than one. They are probably a friend or a family member. If you didn't know this about them, then they were probably worried about how you would react.

Like a lot of the problems we have faced in this country, we have a hard time seeing the other side until it becomes personal. Kids shouldn't be gay until your daughter is and you love her new wife, so now it's okay. Black people shouldn't move into your neighborhood until you have them over for a cookout and you can discuss your favorite sports teams, so now you're happy they live in your neighborhood. Once you see someone as human, it is harder, but unfortunately not impossible, to hate them. Many people are against abortion, but hearing the reason a loved one had it can lead to understanding and sometimes even celebrating the event.

One of the largest problems with talking about this issue is the fact that so much of this conversation is dominated by soundbites that we can simply shout at one another. Politicians do this to gain your vote, and media outlets do this to gain your viewership. Rarely does either one look at the complexities of the issue.

This whole issue was developed to be polarizing and to gain political power and money. Historically, abortion was never a serious crime or a problem. Yes, it was against the law in the U.S. before, but in the sense that it was a misdemeanor, and only if the wife admitted to having gone through the "quickening," i.e., she felt the baby move. So, while it may have been difficult to get, it was only a crime if the wife admitted that she did it. Abortions have been a part of every culture throughout history. Even Southern Baptists were famously pro-choice until recently because the bible instructs people on how to get rid of an unwanted pregnancy (Genesis 2:7) and even says that life begins at first breath (Numbers 5:11-31).

It's easy to call someone a baby killer if you never get to know them or know why they need to get an abortion. It's easy to create a lie that there are "partial-birth" abortions when there is no such thing. We will discuss that point in detail later. It's also easy to believe the lie that science said that life begins at conception if you already believe that it does. Scientists haven't said that. Conversely, it's easy to say that all anti-abortion people want to suppress women and their autonomy while excluding women who are anti-abortion.

However, a funny thing happens when people sit down and talk to each other like human beings about this topic. It is easier for us to listen to each other. We can choose to see each other's perspectives, and we can start to treat each other like thinking and feeling human beings. We must choose to treat each other with respect, and we have to make a choice not to use the platitudes seen during political or media discourse to get out quick comments.

Right now, we are not doing that. There are many ways to lower the need for abortion, but we are not taking any appropriate steps to accomplish it right now. Instead, we are making it harder for women to make decisions that affect their lives and their children's lives.

For example, many states in the U.S. currently allow a rapist to have parental rights to a child conceived by rape. If you can't imagine that, imagine if someone broke into your house. Consequently, they were legally allowed to come into your house whenever they wanted, forever, no matter what house you lived in, and you could do nothing to stop them, or worse, you could even lose your house if you didn't allow them to enter.

Or many states do not allow a child to get an abortion without parental consent. In the case of a child seeking an abortion, this means that they need permission from the same person that is most likely responsible for that child being pregnant.

In both cases, states require victims to continue suffering for their entire lives for a crime committed against them. There is no compassion for life in the decision to do this. There is no concern for autonomy. There is only the desire to control. Also, since the overturn of Roe, these horrific examples have happened. Children have been raped and denied abortions. This is the consequence of denying women a lifesaving medical procedure.

There are ways to lower abortion rates, something that pro-choice people want to do as well. Things like teaching sex education to children and providing healthcare to women lower abortion rates. But laws that punish children and memorialize rapists are not the way to accomplish this.

Imposing religious laws from a loud but narrow branch of one religion upon the entire country are not the right way to do this. Thinking that women do not have control over their entire bodies does not lower abortion rates. Educating women about their bodies and enacting laws that give them autonomy over their bodies is the only means to do this.

Let's tell a story to help illustrate this point. The main point is the need to talk to one another, but as you will see, even when things go wrong, we need to continue talking to one another.

The first time I spoke to a liberal about pro-choice and the intricacies of abortion and its legality, it went very wrong, both in terms of what they wanted to accomplish and what I wanted to learn. This person was, and is, very pro-choice and had had an abortion. Plus, they were very open about this, bringing it up at the oddest times. So, I asked them about it because I wanted to learn more. By the end of the conversation, I was so appalled that I had been staunchly anti-abortion for decades.

I had wished to understand why someone would have an abortion, in what instances it would be permissible, and conversely, which instances would it not. Since this person had an abortion, I thought it would be enlightening. It was, as discussed above, just not in the way they had intended.

As you can imagine, such a conversation would be very disheartening. However, I did not let it quench my desire to learn more about the subject, especially since it is such a divisive topic that affects so many people that I am close with. Since then, I have spoken to more women that have had abortions and have come to empathize with them more.

One takeaway from this story is for the speaker rather than the listener. If someone genuinely asks about this topic, please treat them with the same empathy and respect you ask them to receive the information. Sometimes we can shoot ourselves in the foot without reasoning and empathy. This person I was speaking to was, and is, someone I love dearly and respect, and frankly, on a lot of issues, I still turn to them for advice. However, this conversation did not go as either of us had hoped.

Later in life, my wife and I had trouble conceiving and turned to artificial insemination. The same person above was very happy when we were successful and excited about our few cells, which are now two absolutely wonderful children. Unfortunately, this led to a discrepancy between what we had discussed before and what she was feeling now. Granted, decades had passed, but her opinion on the matter had not changed.

What is my opinion on the matter now? I am currently on the side of women having autonomy over their bodies. What changed my mind? My wife, but not in the way you would expect.

She did not do it solely by making a compelling argument. She did, in fact, make compelling arguments for her stances, which have changed over the years, with good reasons. But I noticed that my opinion of the subject reflected hers when her opinion changed. During the times in her life when she felt one way, I would feel similarly, if not as intensely. Basically, since she was the one that would, and eventually did, bear our children, I placed her opinion on the matter as higher than mine. This led me to the conclusion that I was pro-choice. Not because I did not value life, not because I did not cheer for the potential that I saw on ultrasounds, but because everything that happened with the pregnancy only happened to my wife.

Something to keep in mind is a point that many people I know that are pro-choice or have had abortions have made. It is that no one is pro-abortion. No one wants to be put in the position where they need to make this decision; however, life does not always go as planned. Therefore, they need to be allowed to make the choice that is best for them.

That may be surprising to hear that even the people that are pro-choice are not pro-abortion, but it is true. That's one of the reasons that you need to talk to one another. So, since you have allies in reducing the number of abortions, that is what we will talk about at the end of this section.

However, one question lingers though, what about late-stage abortion? Well, let us think about it. If you have had kids or know someone who has, which I am willing to bet is most of you, what normally happens during the third trimester?

What parties are being thrown? What gifts were bought? What events are planned? What future activities are you thinking about, school, careers, or just having a healthy child? These are pretty good things to think about. It is an exciting time.

Now think about the woman who has to have an abortion late in her pregnancy. How emotionally overwhelming must it be to make that decision? Because of everything I said above, she probably did. For around six months, she knew that a baby was coming and had done everything to prepare for bringing it into the world. But now, she cannot. Do you want the government to get involved in one of the most painful parts of her life?

How much do you want the government involved when you buy a gun? When you go to the doctor, how much do you want the government involved? When are you going through one of, if not the, most painful decision of your life, how much would you get the government involved? I think I know the answer to this. So why do you think we should involve the government to prevent women from making this choice?

I want you to see that women who have abortions are not murderers. They are making a very difficult decision weighing factors we are unaware of. Most of them are already mothers, so they know more about their decisions. Being harassed or assaulted does not help them. Telling them that they are going to hell because of their religious beliefs does not help them.

I can assure you that you know someone that has had an abortion. I know quite a few, and all of their reasons were different. All of them, both the ones that I know and the ones that you know, had to make a choice. All of them deserve care and compassion for the position that they were put in that forced that decision.

We need to have compassion for the people in our lives. They are going through a lot of things; we all are. We need to help one another, work together, and resist the people tearing us apart. Plus, if we want to really care for babies and children. We can do a lot of work together and work on it. Things like ensuring children have food to eat, an education, and a safe place to live.

There are numerous proven ways to lower abortion rates if you are interested in doing that. You can provide education and healthcare to women. If we do not teach boys and girls about their bodies, what do you think will happen when they discover them on their own. They will not know how to care for or protect themselves.

To use a car analogy, we teach kids about basic automotive safety and maintenance from the time they are little so that when they are old enough to drive, they have an understanding and respect for what they are about to do. So why would we not do the same for their bodies?

From listening to women, I know that one thing that may help society understand and accept the need to keep abortion safe and legal is more women sharing that they had an abortion. This would help to normalize it and make it very personal. This argument has a lot of credence; making it personal has helped the LGBTQ+ community become more accepted. When people see their family members are a part of this community, they have a harder time rejecting their humanity. However, that is a very difficult and personal decision that I will never have to make.

Additionally, there will always be people that are more in line with being "forced birth" than they are with educating women. These people care more about the collection of cells inside of a woman than they do her. These are the people that don't want to care for a child after it is born. These are the people that don't want to care for a family. They are by no means "pro-life," but these were never the people I was talking to anyway.

They want to control what a woman does with her uterus. They claim that it doesn't belong to her. They think of pregnancy as a "consequence."

These are not the people I'm writing this section for; I'm writing it for those who may believe that life begins at conception, but that doesn't mean that they should impose their beliefs upon others. This section is to help people realize that if they want to claim to be pro-life, that means a lot more than just making sure a woman gives birth. It means caring for life from the cradle to the grave.

This section is for the people that also believe in religious freedom. For those who believe that we should not inflict our religious beliefs upon one another. People who don't think a small group of people holding a specific religious belief should impose their will on everyone else.

Roe was overturned by a group of dedicated people who felt that their religious beliefs should be imposed upon everyone. Again, no one is really pro-abortion, and there are many people that believe that life begins at conception that still believe abortion should be legal because they believe in people's autonomy. This small group of people have not stopped imposing their religious interpretations upon everyone.

Since overturning Roe, they have already begun to set their sights on making gay and interracial marriage illegal. They have begun targeting the ability of people to even use birth control. This makes them not only forced birth, but forced pregnancy, reducing women to livestock.

This last ask is for the men. We would not want laws that impose upon our bodies, so we have to serve as allies to women in order for them to keep autonomy over their own. We can't look at this as a fight we can ignore. This fight will have consequences on who we can and do love. March along side women for their autonomy. Speak up. Write your representatives.

Chapter Twenty-Nine

Institutional Problems That We Can Fix

It should be obvious by now that we face plenty of institutional problems in making our society better. However, when institutional systems get brought up, people still tend to be confused. Now let us deal with issues we need to address as a society that has to do with our institutional structures. That is because, as we are all aware, institutional changes are slow to take hold. Granted, slow change is by design and not necessarily bad, but when these institutions cause harm, we need to change them.

I do want to take a second and point out a few things. First, while I am specifically addressing the issues facing the United States, I have learned that many other countries face similar institutional problems, some far worse. The news highlights the problems in the U.S., but we are nowhere near the only country facing the problems addressed in this book.

The second is that while I am talking about reforming the institution in the U.S., one thing that doesn't need to be reformed is that this is a rare country that can actually identify an institutional problem without having to worry about going to a reeducation camp or someone putting plutonium in your tea.... you have to love real-life examples that sound like an idea that would be crazy enough for a Bond movie.

Unfortunately, as we have talked about throughout this book, some people feel it is still okay to discriminate against people actively and openly. They see their politicians talk about blacks, Mexicans, Asians, Jews, or anyone that isn't straight and cis-gendered. They see their media reinforce those ideas. Then when they are held to consequence for their actions, they claim to be repressed. Fortunately, there seem to be more people working together, getting involved in civil rights movements, and encouraging us to treat each other humanely.

This is a very recent change in our social thinking that civil rights are important because they affect all of us. It is okay for black people to become police or vote, or not only do we not have to kill gay people, but they can even marry like they are real people. Unfortunately, we still have relics of our previous ways of thinking within our institutional structures. This is where this chapter will focus.

We put into our policies and procedures that we need to police black neighborhoods more frequently, or we teach doctors that black people do not feel pain the same way as white people, or that we give a higher mortgage rate to black home buyers than white ones, or that gender is a binary thing based on parts you are born with. These examples illustrate that even if none of the people involved are racist, sexist, or homophobic, the system itself, the rules that we have to play by, and what we are taught does discriminate against them and prevent them from succeeding. This is what people mean by an institutional problem, like institutional racism. It does not mean that everyone in an institution is racist.

Also, this is another one of the times where I point out that this is not a problem within liberal or conservative areas. The housing rates between blacks and whites in San Francisco, a liberal holy site, provide a wonderful example of the ingrained nature of this within many aspects of our society. This is not something that we can ignore because "my area does not have this problem." It does; now we must fix it.

How do we fix this? That is a good question. I know many people think that we should apply the law equally, and they are correct; that is a good place to start. But many people want to end the progression there. Unfortunately, the problems we are trying to address are that even if there are fair laws and policies on the books, they have not been applied equally for centuries. Additionally, new laws are being enacted that go out of their way to ensure unequal access to opportunities.

In contrast to those that simply want to ignore the problem, when South Africa ended apartheid, it had a Truth and Reconciliation Commission. They looked at the damage caused and allowed people to take an honest look at what happened. Look at Germany, and how, after the Nazi party fell, they taught their future generations about the cause of the war and everything that Germany did wrong during that conflict. They didn't erect monuments to Nazi leaders and hung Nazi propaganda up. They didn't restrict areas where Jews could buy homes and then devalue them. We can follow their example by taking an honest look at our history and reconciling how that has affected our citizens and ingrained problems within our institutions. But like I mentioned in the section on history, we must be honest about what we have done in order to fix it.

To take a quick detour, in researching this book, I have noticed that the laws have been changed in this line of thinking.

Now it is up to the individual, coming up again and again as a reason to not address any of the institutional problems that have remained and that it must be a personal failing on their part that they are unable to succeed.

Here is an example that I am paraphrasing here of why this is a stupid argument. It is the Indy 500, and we will keep it simple by only having two racers. One of them gets a better car and crew and gets to drive for 400 of the 500 miles. Then the other driver, with a worse car and a worse crew, gets to start. Well, now they both have a chance of winning, so if the person that started later does not win, it must be a personal failing on their part. Would you believe that about this race? It may be easy to think that is an over-exaggeration, but many people argue that the losing racer in that example is solely responsible for their failure.

Applying this example to the history and treatment of black Americans, we did not let them own homes until my parent's lifetime. At the same time, white Americans were literally given free land multiple times through Homesteading or were allowed to buy property at much lower rates. Then we said that property taxes funded school systems after we ensured that many black people were relegated to slums, public housing, or near toxic waste (not a euphemism, there are too many black communities that live in these areas still today).

Then we said that they now have access to schooling while obscenely underfunding them, but hey, they now have access, they should be able to do as well as richer schools. Then we pass drug laws that specifically target members of the black and poor communities, which lock up their fathers, and then we get to say that they do not value families because their fathers are not there. So, was the example an over-exaggeration? No, it was not; in fact, it was probably a little too generous. At least I gave the other driver a race car and a pit crew.

Even today, we still devalue housing that is owned by non-white people. There have been lots of cases where the value of a house will go up by half if people think that white people own it. So, these policies are currently in place. Plus, we spoke about policing earlier, but how many times have police officers spoken out about the fact that they are required to make a certain number of stops and that poor neighborhoods are where they can go to make those stops easily?

Hopefully, now we can have a better appreciation for the fact that while, yes, individuals do have a lot of impact on their situation, the environment that they are allowed to play in is also a huge contributing factor. Now, while I did say that most of the laws evened out the playing field, some laws are being passed that outright allow discrimination again. Additionally, while many of these laws have been changed to prevent these practices, the policies in place at these institutions have not caught up. So how about we look at what we can do to address the problem. The first thing that needs to happen is identifying the problem, which I hope we can do not just as a society but as individuals.

As a society, we need to recognize these problems so that they can come to the forefront of our minds. If we do not identify a problem, then there is no hope of fixing it. Besides, many people are working to ensure we never see these problems, like removing enslaved and indigenous people from schoolbooks, much less fixing them. Or passing laws that state we can't learn about history may make us uncomfortable. As individuals, we can see the problems within our own institutions that must be addressed and challenged.

Where are some good places to start? Unfortunately, there are many places where we can get to work. We talked about some of the issues regarding voting and prison reform pertaining to non-white people, and we covered marriage, family, and identity equality pertaining to non-straight cis people. We also covered education as it pertains to everyone. What more could there be? Frankly, more than I am going to include in this book, much less this section.

How about we start with language. How we discuss a problem drastically affects how we see it and, therefore, how we can address it. For a lot of these problems, the first thing that people do is deny they exist. Or they try and justify their discriminatory ideas by saying that these groups of people are morally flawed, that they somehow deserve this, or that keeping them subservient is their "natural state."

Now that we are talking about language let's start with someone like Lee Atwater, who greatly influenced the Republican party during the 1980s and 1990s and spoke about how the language of racism has to change within the country. Mind you, not that he wanted people to stop being racist; he wanted to hide the overt racism so that their policies could have broader appeal. This meant that he, and other politicians, could continue to espouse racist ideas while maintaining plausible deniability. I'm not going to quote him; his language was reprehensible. However, the language he used, that of states' rights, personal responsibility, and protecting the suburbs, is still being used today. On the surface, they seem fine. But recall that the argument around keeping blacks enslaved was reframed to be about states' rights. Plus, if a person is solely responsible for what happens in their life, then society can oppress them as much as possible, and it is their fault for being oppressed. Circular logic is circular. Then there is protecting the suburbs. Protecting them from who? As we discussed earlier, the suburbs were created for white people to flee to get away from non-white people.

Many people use dog whistles, language that appears fine but is heard loud and clear by those that they are speaking to, i.e., racists. Language such as denying the damage that was done to black communities and then saying that it is their fault; they are poor or live in crime-riddled areas. Language such as they are only trying to protect our children, which is why they should be allowed to discriminate against gay and trans people. Or that somehow, after not caring about women's sports, by saying that they should not be paid fairly, worried that trans people are only trying to ruin it. This language is framed so that, on the surface, these statements do not appear harmful. They just want to protect the children, and don't we all want to protect kids. But that does not mean we have to kill trans people or stop them from going to restrooms. If you start to hear language like this, perk up and listen to what they are really trying to get you to agree with. People who use this language hope the listener will slide down that slippery slope into hating their neighbor.

Now that we have tried to clarify that this is an actual problem and some of the language around the problem, we should now talk about the institutional problems holding us back. Because while these problems disproportionately affect some of us, repairing them will help all of us thrive. Why don't we start with housing reform? As many people know, generational wealth can be a huge benefit to people, and preventing them from obtaining it can also be used to keep them down. Earlier, we talked about how blacks, and other people of color, have been actively prevented from buying a home, or once they were able to, it was limited to land no one wanted or was taken away from them. This is not a problem solely in conservative or liberal areas, and this is a problem in both.

On the bright side, we can all work to improve them. If the poor areas in your area are also used to store toxic or dangerous waste, then help to change the policies that allow that, or have the government purchase their land for a reasonable amount. Far too many people in the U.S. have been forced to live next to toxic waste dumps or have had their water poisoned.

Regarding infrastructure, how many homes in the U.S. do not have access to water or sewer? How many have led leaking into their water? How many wells have been polluted by mining or fracking? Fixing these problems helps everyone.

While we are talking about infrastructure, what about broadband internet access? As the recent pandemic illustrated, the internet has become vital to today's ability to conduct business, shop, go to school, and simply interact with one another. Now this problem does affect poor or rural communities more than others. Ensuring access to high-speed internet will allow people to get the resources and personal connections they need more quickly.

We spoke about many problems with the state of education in the U.S. and housing but only briefly mentioned the relationship between the two. A lot of funding for schools comes from property taxes. However, that means that poorer areas tend to have less funding than richer districts. Now, while that may be understandable to a degree, to have a healthy society, we need to have an educated populace. Therefore, ensuring that schools have the resources they need to help us to get there.

There are more issues than what I have covered here, but the important takeaway is that there are still many policies in place that keep people from succeeding. There are laws still being put in place to remove rights from people. So, the narrative that each individual can somehow overcome this all by themselves is false. Plus, in today's society, this doesn't just apply to the groups that I mentioned. If you were not allowed to be yourself, people did not hire you, educate you, or allow you to buy a house or start a company, how far would you go in life? Probably not far, but that is the narrative being told.

Chapter Thirty

Capitalism vs. Socialism

By the title alone, I have no doubt that this section is already raising concerns with many readers. Both terms, capitalism, and socialism, invoke strong emotions in people. This is why I'm going to start by writing about how we hear these words instead of the actual definition.

Now, before I go too far down this path, I want us all to remember that this book is trying to get us to listen to one another, which I hope by this point is a little easier. There is a lot that is said on this topic that upsets a lot of people, and frankly, there is a lot that should be worrisome about both.

Okay, is everyone ready to get upset at me? Yes? Good, then let's get started.

When some people hear the word socialism, they think of things like China, the Soviet Union, and Venezuela. They think of every time a country uses the language of socialism to seize control of production and install dictators. They think of every time this has been used to oppress a population.

Now, their concerns about those countries I listed are valid. There are lots of problems with their governments and the rights that they suppress. But again, those countries used the language of socialism (power to the people; freedom from government oppression; equal opportunity) to install a dictatorship masquerading as communism. No power is given to the people, dissent is quelled in the harshest ways, and there are very few individual freedoms.

Or these same people think about European countries. They think about how these countries have big plans, but their economies are perceived as not moving forward at the same pace as the U.S. Their media tells them that these countries lack innovation and that their economies have become stagnant and complacent, even if it is not true for these countries. For people that have seen the decline of numerous industries in the U.S., this is a worrisome concern.

These people hear the label "socialism" being used by their media and politicians as a fear word to scare them away from any progress. This word has been used as a fear word throughout U.S. history to prevent us from instituting any policy that may, or removing those that do, help people. The 40-hour work week, roads, police and fire departments and public education were some of the issues described as socialist before they were implemented. Many of the programs and policies that were used to create the middle class were removed because of the label "socialism."

Conversely, when people hear the word capitalism, they think of all the times the economy has collapsed in recent decades. They think of the Great Recession, the Housing Crisis, bailouts for businesses that are "too big to fail," or the simple fact that many regular people lost their jobs during the pandemic while rich people got significantly richer.

They think of things like significant droughts caused in the southwestern U.S. because companies have taken all the water from those regions. They think of the recent freezes in Texas and the deaths caused because it was cheaper for industries not to winterize their power plants. They think of these centibillionaires who spend lots of money on rockets while refusing to pay their workers a living wage or provide benefits.

They have seen a government that provides socialism for the rich by bailing them out and providing them numerous incentives and tax breaks. Then conversely, the same government expects a "rugged capitalism" for everyone else, expecting them to get out of their own dilemmas and simply find new jobs and housing.

This is all supported by a media that says if you want better than starvation wages, you should just find a new job. The same media calls these people lazy for not wanting to work for starvation wages instead of calling out employers for not paying high enough wages. People see a system actively working against them, and they are growing tired of it.

All those collapses and bailouts have happened in the past decade, which means that many younger voters have been seeing rich people and corporations getting bailed out, and the same people that caused the problem getting rewarded with golden parachutes instead of arrested when there is a financial crisis. They see the inequity in the system, and they are tired of it.

They see that our current version of capitalism is not working. They see themselves burdened with a debt that previous generations never saw. They see home values being artificially inflated beyond what they can afford, which was already past what previous generations paid.

They see the cost of their education going up solely to keep them in debt for longer. They see that they are going to go into debt with any medical crisis that comes upon them. They see a system that has been designed to keep them from being successful.

Plus, they see that this system is different from the ones their parents and grandparents had. They see that their parents had more affordable education and that they were able to buy their own homes. They see that they could get a good job with just a high school education. They are understandably tired of the current system of capitalism in our country and want to change it.

I want to make a point here, but I think it would be best illustrated if we took a break for a quick story time. This time it will be a fairy tale, The Boy Who Cried, Wolf. Once upon a time, there was a boy who lived in a village that was supposed to be watching over the sheep. One day, being bored, he came running to the village crying that a wolf was attacking the sheep.

This spurred the villagers to band together and headed off to the fields to protect their livestock, which the boy found very entertaining. So, he decided to do it again and got similar results. Again, the villagers came out, and he had a great time watching everyone running around.

But the villagers noticed that there were no wolves and were becoming very angry at and distrustful of the boy. So much so that wolves attacked the flock one day, and no one believed him when the boy ran to the villagers.

Why was this story relevant? Well, the moral of the story is that if you keep lying, sooner or later, people will stop believing you or just disregard you together. This is relevant because there are so many people screaming in the media and some of our social media feeds that if we implemented any of the policies we used to have in place, that would be a turn towards socialism.

If you start calling everything socialism, it begins to lose all meaning in public discourse. Plus, it means that the people being hurt by today's policies have begun to look back at the policies in place for previous generations and think that "socialism" did work in our country. So instead of scaring people away from socialism, this discourse is marching them towards adopting it.

I know that socialism is a very effective political scare word. People hear that, and they get very nervous, but at some point, it loses that effectiveness, like I think it has with the younger population. If you call roads, schools, the fire department, electricity, water, basic infrastructure, social security, and Medicare socialism, then people will naturally think socialism is good.

This is where we turn from talking about what people think when hearing about the other side to the systems we're dealing with and where people want to go. To be clear, we will be talking about the form of capitalism within the U.S., not the forms that exist elsewhere in the world. This form of capitalism only exists here, and capitalism is not exclusive to the U.S. Many other countries practice their own form of it.

Even within the U.S., we have different styles of capitalism, with their own strengths and weaknesses. For comparison, let's look at California and Texas. Both are capitalist economies, but they both take different views on taking care of their citizens. Each of them does some things right, and both do some things that hurt their citizens.

California has a fairly left-leaning population. As such, they do some decent things like ensuring that childcare is available for their workers, and they provide massive investments for startup companies. Alternatively, they have taxes that are so repressive, especially once you get to a local level, that they are forcing people and companies to move out of the state. Additionally, the cost of housing is so high there that people can spend over 50% of their monthly income on rent, and they have one of the highest homeless populations in the country.

Alternatively, there is Texas, whose tax and housing policies have made them a ripe location for companies, and the people that work for them, to resettle. But unfortunately, they have problems with not providing enough government oversight, which has recently bitten them a few times, especially regarding their power grid.

For those that do not know, the power grid in Texas is not a part of the national network because they do not want to be regulated. This, in and of itself, is not a bad thing, but while regulation and government oversight, like with California, can become a hindrance, a complete lack of regulation and government oversight is also a problem, as we will discuss.

Because of climate change, Texas has begun to suffer crippling winter storms with a far greater frequency. During those storms, their electrical grid goes down, and if the weather is bad enough, like what happened in the winter of 2021, then people die.

When this happened, politicians and the media were quick to blame all sorts of things, like windmills and solar panels being unable to work in the cold. Despite windmills being used in Antarctica and solar panels being used in space, both places are far colder than Texas.

Spoiler, it was not the cold, but because Texas was so opposed to regulations, they did not insulate their power grid against cold weather, leading it to fail. They knew it was a problem, but they did not want any regulations, so they never addressed the issue

More specifically, they knew they could make far more money by not regulating and insulating the grid. How? Because Texas operates its power grid on a supply and demand structure. This means that when a storm shuts down parts of the electrical grid and demand increases, they could charge a lot more for the electricity being generated. Basically, these companies decided they would make way more money by not fixing these problems. Please remember that the decision not to fix these problems resulted in hundreds of deaths and electrical bills in the tens of thousands. It's also not the first time this has happened in Texas.

When capitalism and socialism are discussed by our politicians or within our media, they provide us with a distorted view of our choices. We either need to have unregulated capitalism and go back to having company towns where a corporation owns us, or we need everything controlled by the government. That we will either tax people and companies out of the state or that we need to deregulate to the point where it literally kills people.

There is plenty of ground between those extremes. This is why U.S. citizens have started to look at how the citizens in Europe and Canada have changed their relationship with government and business. They see what is working there, and if we lay claim to being the greatest, they wonder, rightfully so, why we can't have that here.

There are plenty of good discussions to be had about how much the government is allowed to regulate citizens or private corporations. But when people see environmental disasters being committed by BP, which is fined for less than a quarter of the damage they caused. The same company that tries to blame ordinary citizens for climate change. When companies like Nestle say that water isn't a right and should all be privatized. When they see drug prices skyrocketing beyond what people can pay. When companies are allowed to contaminate groundwater without consequence, they see that our current version of capitalism isn't working.

We need to think about what role we want for our government and how it relates to the rest of the citizens. Right now, our economic system is set up for the wealthy (e.g., continued bailouts and lack of substantive negative consequences) and rugged capitalism (e.g., lack of safety net, and holding them responsible for their success in an environment for which they have no control) for everyone else is not working. Fortunately, this is becoming more and more obvious. Because then we can take the actions to change our circumstances.

Do we want to ensure that there is a floor for people, so they do not become homeless or destitute? Do we want to ensure that our drinking water is free of lead and other harmful chemicals? Do we want to sell all our water instead of having access to it?

Should our energy infrastructure be regulated to handle major storms, especially since they are becoming more frequent? Should there be lead in our pipes or our paint? What about asbestos? Should we have to pay a loan with a 29% interest rate? We can come to a happy medium with enough regulation to ensure people's health and well-being without destroying business (again, please see the argument earlier that everything because you call something socialism does not make it true).

We can come to a happy medium between these ideas. We are a government of the people, for the people. But right now, we have a government that is actively working against its people because we are no longer holding it accountable.

We first need to support one another in our efforts to improve our situations. This book covered a lot of work that needs to get done, but it can be done together and by helping each other organize, whether that be to get the pay and benefits that we are owed as workers or whether we are organizing to hold our government accountable.

In our history, we have taken care of our people while going through periods of extreme economic growth. However, we did have strong social programs and legislation in place during those times. Therefore, it is not an either/or proposition. We need not let fear guide us, but we must pursue our dreams for the future.

These dreams united us and allowed us to accomplish more than any of us could accomplish alone. We have tackled huge problems like acid rain or the hole in the ozone. We can tackle climate change. We used to go to other planets, but instead, we have been shrinking the budget for NASA and letting billionaires take over the space race. If there was no innovative reason to invest in space, then why are there so many billionaires with their own space companies?

Some European countries have been derided as socialist by our media, innovating more frequently than we do currently. However, we can return to being an innovative society that ensures our citizens have a future. That's what most of us are asking for, the freedom to have choices about our future.

Chapter Thirty-One

Moving Forward

A conservative friend of mine, who I will always love and respect, no matter how much I argue with him, would always say that you need to tell people what you are going to tell them, tell them, and then repeat what you told them. This is the part of the book where I repeat myself.

For reference's sake, he and I worked together for many years, and there were many meetings in which we would yell at each other, much to the discomfort of our peers and bosses, but we never forgot the important part. We were both fighting about different ways to save the lives of soldiers. We were generally arguing about how it should be done or the cause of death, but we were both there with the same goal in mind, so it did not matter that we disagreed. I still liked him, and I think he still likes me; we will see after this book comes out.

The point of the story is that we can argue, and we can argue passionately and vigorously, but we need to remember that we are on the same team. We are, in many ways fighting for the same things. Unfortunately, many people want to use that perceived rift and turn us against one another. They want to use that argument to make it seem like we do not like each other or that we disagree, or that we are un-American. In the story I told above, people knew the two of us; they knew we were both passionate, and they knew that we both wanted to make sure that the right thing was done in the right way. Therefore, any argument was okay. We do not all see eye to eye on every problem, and we do not have to either.

First, there are lots of people that want to take advantage of any perceived difference that we may have and exploit it for their own means. Politicians want to take advantage of political power and influence, and the media wants to sensationalize it to increase their consumers and get more money. There is a lot of money to be made by telling us that we do not like one another, that one side is trying to eat babies, or that the other is all racist. Again, I wish that was a euphemism.

Hold your politicians accountable. There have been several Supreme Court cases that have enabled nearly unlimited money to go to politicians from corporations; therefore, they are more likely to listen to them. That is unless the will of the people is strong enough to convince them otherwise. We all agree that money should get out of politics and that the unlimited money idea is bad. We all both agree that there should be term limits. So let's work together to make this a reality.

The media loves to get our attention. They crave it; their headlines and story placement are designed to get us to read or watch. Remember the old adage that "man bites dog" sells the story? The same still applies today, but the information constantly bombards us can become desensitized to sensational media. This puts them in the position that they have to be really outlandish to get our attention.

Unfortunately, this leads to so many people believing crazy things are happening in our world that isn't, or conversely, are never told about the crazy things happening. If you rely only on one type of media and never bring up information, then they can prevent us from knowing and engaging on a subject. We no longer will have a common set of facts that we can use to talk about.

Therefore, you should diversify your media sources. See what conservative media is saying, see what liberal media is saying, and see what the sources that just report facts without interpretation are saying, like the Associated Press. What are foreign news sites saying? See what other news agencies are reporting on to give yourself a new perspective. This will help you get out of the bubble that you are in. It will help you see what information the other side is being told, which will help you understand their perspective. If any media outlet tells us that the other side is destroying the country, we should probably turn it off.

Social media can be a good thing, but it can really hinder us in many ways. There are friends I have been able to stay in touch with thanks to social media that otherwise I would have never heard from again. I am able to stay in contact with the coworker I mentioned before because of social media. Social media allowed me to become much better friends with someone I knew in high school, who is also one of the people I am getting to review this book. Social media allowed these things to happen.

On the flip side, it allows people, myself included, to create a bubble of information. I get to choose what types of information I get exposed to, and then these sites can change what advertisements I see, furthering my bubble. I am using me as an example, but this applies to all of us. Most people do the same thing as well. However, we need to make sure that we burst these bubbles.

Think about what you want from these social media platforms. Think about what you get from them. Do you still get joy from them? Know that keeping a bubble of information can be dangerous. We have seen the dangerous effects that staying within a bubble leads to. We have seen lots of our friends corrupted by these bubbles. Do not become like that. If you see your friends becoming like that, help them see the way out. Show compassion towards them. If they start down a toxic path and you need to remove yourself from that relationship, then do. Show compassion towards yourself.

So, let's start with the things we can work together that I would like us to take away from this book, and I will move through these like I did through the book. First and foremost, do not place yourself solely in one box. I know many people who would be considered a liberal who love and own guns, and I know conservatives who do not. All because you primarily fit into one box does not mean that you need to fit all of your beliefs into there. The spectrum of thoughts and ideas within this country is limitless, don't confine yourself or others to a simple box.

The second thing is that we must realize that everyone who disagrees with us is not our enemy. All because they have different ideas for improving the country does not inherently make them bad people. If we work together on a topic, we will find that we can get the right thing done in the right way.

A few topics that can be vastly improved by working together are Environmental reform, Healthcare, and Gun Rights. These are hugely important topics to each of us and need to be addressed in the right way in order to move forward. Conservatives led a lot of efforts to establish the Environmental Protection Agency and eliminate the hole in the ozone layer. Plus, we all agree that we need to ensure that there are jobs for people as we move away from the technologies of the 18th and 19th centuries.

For healthcare, again, there are lots of good points on either side. We do need to ensure that people have access to healthcare. We need to ensure that our healthcare expenses do not go up because people can not afford care. We also need to make sure that we as a country can argue for the prices of medicine so that we no longer subsidize other countries. Lastly, we must make sure we can innovate and provide the best quality care. A mixture of ideas seems to be the only way to make this work. I do not know exactly what that looks like, but conservative and liberal leaders have tried ways to make this work. We need to ensure that they work together on these solutions so we all win.

For gun rights, we should work together to define them. Like I said, it has only been since 2008 since we had an individual right to bear arms. But even in that decision, they said that limits could be placed. So, we can work together to define those limits and terms. No right is without limits, and that makes sense too. But if the only argument coming to the table is "no," then the moment people have enough votes for a "yes, " they will be the ones defining those limits. So, work together to help make laws that make sense.

For the larger issues, this will take real work by everyone. In addition to the great things that they did, our forefathers worked hard to ensure that there were institutional inequities in our society that we have been addressing ever since. The first thing we have to do is understand our history, how it was rewritten, and how all of this has affected our present. Then we can begin working on the hard stuff. Once we have identified these inequities, we can work toward repairing them.

Hopefully, we have moved past the point where it is okay for normal citizens to murder people based upon the way they were born, whether by skin color, gender, or orientation. But that time is not that far back in our history. Because of that, many of our institutions are still built upon the belief that it is acceptable for certain groups to be treated negatively or even murdered. Now we have to undo all those enshrined policies, which is what they mean by institutional racism, but it applies more broadly.

The next thing that we need to do is hold our politicians more accountable. We all agree that the government should be by and for the people, and we all seem to agree that it currently is not. Additionally, we all like the idea of getting money out of politics and making term limits for politicians. We all also want transparency in who is donating to certain politicians. I love the joke that politicians should wear outfits similar to NASCAR drivers that advertise who has paid for their campaign. That way, people have transparency with the people they are voting into office. However, both parties are adamant about keeping money in their pockets and staying in power for as long as possible. We all want transparency in our elected officials.

So do what we can to vote out the people that are not representing our interests. Vote in the people that do. We absolutely can make sure that the government is accountable to us. Every time that either one of you protests, something happens. It should not always have to come to that, but when it does, do not be afraid to stand up for what you believe. We are all frustrated that the government is not working for the people; we have an ally with the people that disagree with us on policy implementation.

Lastly, and not to sound too "Pollyanna," there is a lot that we can do together. We need to recognize the basic humanity in one another. We need to see that there are people out there hurting. We need to help take care of one another. We need to reach out because we have more allies than we realize. Stop letting people tear us apart.

About Author

Sean earned a BA from Appalachian State University and then spent the next few years as a counsellor and a social worker. He then spent four years in the U.S. Air Force and was deployed with the Army to Mosul in 2006. After getting out of the Air Force, he went to work for the Army, where he has been since. He is a Unitarian Universalist with a Master's degree in Strategic Intelligence. This dichotomy means that at work, he is regarded as a liberal, whereas at church, he is seen as one of the conservatives.

Acknowledgments

Thank you to Jenn, Nikki, Corrina, Katie, Terrance, Nick, Carla, Sam, and Steve for proofreading this book and helping me talk about subjects I could never experience.

www.ingramcontent.com/pod-product-compliance
Lightning Source LLC
Chambersburg PA
CBHW070104030426
42335CB00016B/2007
9798986672526